MOTHERS BEFORE

Mothers Before

STORIES AND PORTRAITS
OF OUR MOTHERS
AS WE NEVER SAW THEM

by EDAN LEPUCKI

Abrams Image, New York

Contents

Introduction

Mothers are difficult to describe—or at least mine is.

I try to tell people what my mom is like: That she possesses an unwavering confidence in her parenting, as she should, having raised five children and helped to take care of six grandchildren as well as various kids who aren't related to her. That she loves to read fiction, all kinds, from the commercial to the turgid. That she wears diamond earrings the size of raisins but grew up sharing one bathroom with her parents and five siblings in a blue-collar New Jersey town. That in high school she designed some of her own clothing and, for nearly my whole life, collected beautiful shoes, but that she now prefers to wear her no fuss "cooking" T-shirts and has become pathologically devoted to FitFlops.

My mother is efficient and practical. She is content and perpetually optimistic. She doesn't curse. She giggles at her own jokes. She never loses control. She can prepare a meal for fifteen while maintaining her kitchen's spotlessness. She will tell you about various hotel lounges even after you've said the descriptions are too boring to bear. She has traveled the world and, because iced tea isn't an international phenomenon, knows how to ask for hot tea with ice cubes in about ten languages. Even a recent fall in Poland, which required stitches to her forehead, has not dampened her wanderlust. She will talk to strangers everywhere. She is the least judgmental person I know, particularly about her children. She has never expected me to be anyone but who I am.

Maybe because I'm a novelist, I've long wished I could write a fictional version of my mother that truly captures her complicated essence. But I can't. Even this list of details barely scratches the surface of who she is. Whatever I wrote would be a paper doll compared to my real mother. There's so much to her!

In 2015, however, I *did* publish a novel that featured mother-daughter relationships, called *Woman No. 17*, though it wasn't a depiction of my own relationship with my mom. To promote the book, I decided I would create an Instagram account that invited women and nonbinary people to share photos of their mothers before they became mothers. Their captions, just a couple of sentences long, would tell us about their mom: about the image of her, or about what's occurred in the decades since the shutter opened, then closed. They would tell us how they felt about their mother. The project, I hoped, would offer glimpses of this most seminal relationship, whether it be easy or fraught or beautiful or damaged or intimate or distant or all of that at once.

The Instagram account, which shares the same title as this book, showcases all kinds of mothers, from the mysterious to the consistent, from the cruel to the saintly. There are mothers across many eras and many countries. The lives recounted are fascinating, as are the daughters' feelings. The account became its own work of art, unrelated to my novel. It was more popular than I imagined it would be, and when I got the opportunity to take the premise of the Instagram account and transform it into a book, I was excited because I knew the expanded format would provide me with new perspectives on the project.

Since the Instagram account's inception, I've thought a lot about why it has captured people's attention. Honestly, I shouldn't have been surprised by its popularity. I'm not only a daughter, I'm also a mother myself, and I am deeply interested in how this relationship shapes how we perceive ourselves. It's why I wrote my novel, I suppose. But my fascination is not uncommon. We all want to know about one another's mothers: the ways she nurtured you or failed you. How her death changed you. Her piece of tossed-off advice that you will never forget. Perhaps, most importantly, how that story of her as a young woman has followed you around your whole life. Did it serve as inspiration? A cautionary tale? A riddle?

What I've come to realize about this project is that it's not only about motherhood and the mother-daughter relationship; it's also, at its heart, about representing the female experience in all its complexity and shedding light on the limited ways we might, as daughters and as a society, interpret that experience. How daughters talk about their mothers before they became mothers illustrates what we value in women—younger women, specifically, or, even, exclusively.

As I wrote in the *New York Times* about the project, "Pluck, sex appeal, power, kindness, persistence: We admire and celebrate these characteristics, and we long for the past versions of our moms to embody them. But if these characteristics are a prerequisite for a properly executed womanhood, does becoming a mother divest a woman of such qualities?" When motherhood is a part of a woman's narrative, it often becomes a before-and-after dividing line. Looking closely at an old photo of your own mother and asking yourself who she was then, and who she is now, asks you to blur that line a little. To take in the whole of her life, the whole of her self. This, in turn, allows us to do the same for our own lives and selves.

I gave the talented contributors of this collection very few parameters: Send me a photo of your mom and write about it in 100 to 800 words. I hoped these micro-essays would capture not only a mother's life but a specific way to read that life, for we can't disconnect these stories from their tellers. I wanted this fact to be central to the book. As daughters, we are always reading our mothers, and our perspective will always be both flawed and privileged. We are too close to the subject, not nearly neutral enough, we've got too much skin in the game—and, because of this, our gaze is powerful.

Between the covers of this book are images of elegance, gumption, innocence, knowingness, frailty, naivete, willfulness, beauty, strength, resilience, vulnerability, triumph—and more. What came into focus for me as I read the pieces that accompanied these images was how much work it takes to connect with our mothers before. It takes respect and compassion to consider the woman we will never get to know and to try and square her with the woman we do know, and to accept that not all the discrepancies will be resolved. For some of the contributors, their experience of reading their mothers is a celebration. For others, it's a reckoning. Either way, it's work. It's an effort of love.

These pieces also shed light on how we cannot wrest a person from her circumstances or the facts of her identity. As Jennifer Egan writes, "I sometimes wonder what kind of life my mother would have had if she'd been born ten, or even five, years later." Haven't we all considered how our mothers were molded by the gender constraints of their eras? In Egan's case, her mother's looks dictated her trajectory: "My mom is a beautiful woman," she writes, "and in 1950s America, beauty like hers must have felt like destiny."

Gender is just one facet of experience for many of these mothers. In her piece, Camille T. Dungy writes of her family's roots in Lynchburg,

Virginia: "The members of Court Street Baptist Church started a library fund to help my black mother's black father buy the books he needed to preach the sermons his black parishioners needed to hear every Sunday in that deeply segregated, often hateful town." The repetition of "black" is instructive here: Dungy doesn't separate race from historical fact because they're inextricable, as is the racism that pervaded her mother's childhood. Dungy's piece reminds us that the outside world—for many an inhospitable, cruel place—will make its way into our personal lives. However, like Egan, Dungy acknowledges that her mother thrived despite these circumstances; in the photo, she recognizes "the origins of my mother's deep pride and joy: her sense of connection with the people who love her and whom she loves."

This theme of resilience, of thriving nevertheless, persists throughout the book. Paria Kooklan and Eirene Donohue, among other contributors, consider how national upheaval and war changed the course of their mothers' lives. Their pieces acknowledge the losses their mothers experienced, and yet, they also assert that essential aspects of their mothers' personalities, some untouchable core, remain.

Many contributors remark on the choices our mothers made for the benefit of their children. Jia Tolentino wonders how her mother's "willingness to place love over personal ambition" has allowed Jia personal and professional freedoms she might not have had otherwise. Dana Spiotta wrestles with why her mother stopped acting when she married and became a mother. As daughters, we are keenly aware of the sacrifices our mothers made in our names: If our lives are less constrained than theirs were, it's because of the opportunities they fought to give us. But in providing us with these opportunities, what did they have to forgo? As I read this book, I kept asking myself if motherhood requires a woman to surrender, to sacrifice. Does a *giving to* signify a *giving up*? Or will that be a vestige of a bygone time when women had fewer choices? Then again, perhaps my interpretation is too narrow. As Dana Spiotta comes to realize about her own mother's path: "Potential is hers to keep."

Paging through this book, I realize that this project is so much deeper than I initially imagined. It's more than sepia tones and miniskirts and killer legs (though that's all here, too, of course). It's about seeking clarity, and interrogating history, and trying to understand the myriad ways a woman might navigate a life.

*

Circa 1999

As I type this, my third child swims around in my uterus, a couple months shy of being born. What will he make of me when he is older? My only daughter is three-and-a-half and already we have conflicts: I will not let her wear fancy shoes to the park; she does not like when I hurry her through the mundane tasks of living; when I went away for a week to write she told me over the phone, "I want you back."

I worry that she and her brothers will remember me as being too distracted, too taken with my work, too quick to anger about things of no consequence. Will they realize how many appointments I drove them to, how many fruit bowls I cut up, how I gazed at their beauty, moony eyed with love? I hope not, or rather, I hope not yet: While they are young, I want my children to have the privilege of taking me for granted. I want my efforts to be invisible to them—just as my mother's once were to me.

And yet, I also want to be seen for myself. I am a mother, and it's a crucial part of my life and identity, but it's not everything. Will my kids eventually understand how much I loved to write, how dancing made me feel, that I loved a dirty joke, a good cappuccino? Will they be able to imagine me before—and beyond—them?

They will certainly have more photos of my youth to inspect than I have of my own mother's. But that also gives me pause. As it gets easier and easier to snap pictures, as each of us amasses more and more digital evidence of our past, perhaps coming upon an old image will feel less like discovering a precious artifact, so full of mystery, its subject only partially legible. If my children decide to have children, their offspring may find that the vast archive of digital images is far too exhaustive, or far too curated, to be revelatory. My kids' generation might be the last to experience the power of old photos. While there are still boxes of physical pictures in our garage for them to dig through, I'm not sure how many mothers who come after me will be able to say the same. In this way, *Mothers Before* feels even more poignant: a record of what it's like to be an adult daughter now, in this era, straddling the analog and the digital.

I do know that my daughter loves to flip through my photo albums from high school, college, and graduate school. I wonder what she, specifically, sees when she looks at these old pictures. Often when we tell stories about things that happened years ago—when our dog was a puppy, or when her brother was a baby—she asks, "Where was I? But where was I?" as if, in every narrative, she's simply in another room or at school. She can't yet imagine a world that doesn't include her.

When she's older, though, and she goes through those boxes of photos, what will she think? I wonder if she will flip through them and see me. Will she recognize my goofiness, my innocence, my mischief, my ambition?

If she does, I hope she will feel comforted.

If she doesn't, if parenthood has rendered me a different creature altogether, I hope the disruption will at least give her pause and allow her to deliberate on her own life and how she might have changed or stayed the same.

And then I hope she snatches all that mischief and ambition for herself. And never lets them go.

My mother at sixteen looks wiser than I am at sixty. Sophisticated and poised, too, in a way that I clearly never will be. Extremely thin, something else I will never be. Although I was a preemie, barely five pounds at birth, I gained weight rapidly; soon, my arms and legs were so deeply creased they looked like little pans of break-apart rolls ready for the oven. My grandmother counted the folds in my thighs and noticed that one side had more than the other. A doctor was consulted, and he said that one hip was slightly higher. "If she were a boy, I might correct it," the doctor said, "but it's fine for a girl to walk with a twitch."

When my mother turned sixteen, World War II was not even two years in the past. She had spent part of the war on the coastal island of St. Simons, where her mother and aunt shared a house. They thought the children would be safer there than in Atlanta. My father lived on the Georgia mainland, in Brunswick; my mother went to school there, knew his cousins. But they would not meet for almost another decade, when he returned from the Korean War and enrolled in graduate school at Emory. My mother was a secretary to one of the deans, and when she announced her plans to marry Ted Lippman, her boss pulled my future father's confidential record and said, "You can't marry him. Look at this! And this! *And this*."

I don't know what details the dean shared with my mother, and she no longer remembers. She did, however, often tell me this: "I could have married richer men. But I never could have married a more interesting one."

I took that as advice.

LAURA LIPPMAN

1947

S ure, everyone *likes* to make a connection with an animal, but few people *love* it the way my mother loves it. And most animals want to hang out with her, too.

Here's one of her favorite moments: Once, at the Monterey Bay Aquarium, my mother had a long interaction with an otter that kept swimming up with different toys and presenting them to her for inspection. When it ran out of toys, it swam back one final time and *waved good-bye*. I was there. So were my sister and father. But the otter didn't pay attention to any of us—it was focused solely on my mother.

We've reminisced fondly about that moment so often you'd think we were actually related to the otter.

In this photo I love the way the goat is nestled against my mother like they're friends, even though they could only have just met. It was taken at the petting zoo section of Six Flags in Missouri, which she visited with my dad when they were both graduate students at Illinois State in Normal, Illinois; my parents grew up in Taipei, but they didn't meet until they both came here for graduate school. I love all the photos of them dressed in impeccable seventies style, getting soaked at Niagara Falls or road-tripping through the Petrified Forest, but this one is my favorite because of the way my mom is smiling and looking so purely happy to be there with that baby goat. She still has an ageless ability to be thoroughly delighted by things. I love that about her, and I like to think it's a trait that, thanks to her, my entire family shares.

JADE CHANG

1970s

1960

don't know where this photo was taken, or by whom, but this is my mom, Jill, cracking up, boldly and beautifully. Her laugh was recognizable—and loud! You could hear her howls ring down halls and through elevator shafts (not unlike her daughter's). She was quick to roar with glee about something funny she'd said or snicker over something witless a politician had done. Many years after this photo was taken, she laughed merrily with my sister and me as we sat around the kitchen table, where she held a new head-of-the-household position. Later, she giggled with joy when hearing of something a grandchild accomplished. And later still, with a combination of frailty and fate, she dissolved into laughter as she gamely faced her lung cancer prognosis and treatment. Her ability to find the funny in all of life's pains and detours is only one of many lessons I draw from, especially on days when I feel her loss most acutely.

FRAN MELMED

There is such fragility in this image of my mother, who would develop schizophrenia in her late teens or early twenties, gave me the sort of childhood that either strengthens or kills a kid, and died in the state psychiatric hospital at age fifty-seven.

SHARON SMITH

Early 1920s

1964

My grandfather took this snapshot of my mother, Patricia, shortly after her high school graduation ceremony in 1964. I think she looks so crisp and fresh in her navy blue-and-white dress, her hair perfectly flipped, against the greenery of the football field. In a few months, she would attend Hampton Institute (now Hampton University), a historically black college in Virginia, where my grandfather and great-grandfather had studied. Her high school graduation continued a long tradition of academic excellence in our family, and the lightness and precision of this photograph parallel my sense of those expectations. Education is everything in my family. My mother became a teacher and, later, an instructional specialist in Baltimore City Public Schools. Her grace and kindness, which you can see in her beautiful smile, made her a favorite among students. To this day, whenever I return with her to the Baltimore area, I witness how these same students—now all grown up—regularly recognize my mother, calling her name across museum lobbies, over the railings of escalators, or around the corners of restaurant booths, to thank her for everything she taught them. Now that I'm a university professor, I realize that I've arrived here because of my mother's strength, her commitment to every element of the learning process, her curiosity about the lives of others, and her incredible heart.

KIKI PETROSINO

Early 1990s

This photograph was taken in Kenya when my mother was probably twenty or twenty-one. She's the one in white. I have always loved this photo. Her demeanor, cool and collected, looking far off in the distance. Her clothing. That subtle cross of her feet. The bottle of Coca-Cola in her hand. It's hard to believe my mother, or any of our mothers, really, had lives before they had us. How strange . . .

VALLERIE MWAZO

The first time I saw this photograph, I thought it was of me. I was outside the post office on my college campus, nineteen or twenty, when I tore open the envelope and saw a photo tucked inside my grandmother's usual monthly letter. I remember how I gasped, standing there straddling my bike, when I realized that the face I was looking at wasn't mine but my mother's. I let out a sob, I remember: that's how shocked I was, how confused. There was a date stamped on the back of the photo: December 1968, ten years before I was born. Her hair was short and frosted, much brassier than her natural dark brown. Her mouth hung open like mine does when I'm not thinking about it, as though a fishing sinker were tied to my lower lip. I'd never seen her look so blank, so wide-open, so sort of lost. I'd never seen us look so much alike.

My mother has always seemed like she knew her way, even when she couldn't have. She was one of a family of seven children, the third-oldest. The family began to collapse in the late eighties—first a brother's death to AIDS, then a sister to cancer, and on and on—and now, at seventy-two, she's lost both parents and five of her six siblings. She bolstered herself by getting into therapy in the late eighties, before it seemed like a mainstream thing. I can still see the *Codependent No More* desk calendar propped on the counter of my childhood kitchen. My mother has worked hard, in her quiet and elegant way, to keep going. She cared for her identical twin sister through a losing battle with pancreatic cancer in 2012. She'd done the same for my father ten years before, when he was felled by metastatic kidney cancer. She became a widow at fifty-six.

And yet she's out in the world, fit and energetic, reading Lauren Groff and teaching Pilates, as she has for more than two decades. Three years ago, she moved from Oklahoma City to Seattle and into a house a block from mine. Her days are full enough, and my days are full enough, that sometimes we go all week without seeing each other, except when we carpool on Sunday mornings to the high-intensity dance

1968

workout class we both love. She'll come for dinner with a bottle of sauvignon blanc that she wants to try, a new recommendation from the wine guy at Trader Joe's.

I worry I should see her more, take fuller advantage of our proximity. I never forget that I will lose her. But this feels like us, the rhythm we've got. I know it is rare and lucky, as an adult woman, to get to see my mother this way: thriving, still adapting, as living proof of what is possible. I'm trying to memorize her while I can.

MOLLY WIZENBERG

1945

My mother, Nancy, was almost nineteen when this photo was taken in 1945. She always said it was fun after the war ended, but I was still surprised to see her posing at the Jersey Shore with two soldiers she'd only just met! They appear to be standing on the seawall. I love her pin-up bathing suit. Seeing this picture reminds me of my own bikini-wearing teen adventures at the Jersey Shore.

Later, Mom graduated nursing school and met my father at the hospital where they both worked. She loved being a nurse but stayed home after my brother (the first of six kids) was born. I think her life was harder than she imagined it would be: a lot of work and financial struggles. As a mother, though, she appreciated us for who we were. I think I'm the same with my own kids. She gave us all a love for children—especially babies—and taught us how to care for others.

She returned to nursing when she was in her forties, after my youngest sister went to preschool. In her late fifties, she retired to the mountains of North Carolina, where she joined the mountain rescue team and fire department!

I bet my mom dove into the ocean the day this photo was taken. I bet she swam very far out, just as she did when I was a kid. I used to worry she would be swept out to sea. She had a daring, adventurous side that I caught only in glimpses.

MARGARET GUZIK

Here is my mother, Susan, working as a copyboy at the *Chicago Tribune* in the early 1970s. At that time, women were scarce in newsrooms, hence the job title. She had to promise in her interview that she wouldn't cry at work! Indeed, she didn't, and continued to work in journalism for the next thirty years. The picture was taken by my father. The *Tribune* was where they met.

KATE CRUM

Early 1970s

Mid- to late-1960s

've wondered about this photo. It's a strange one to have survived over fifty years and made its way to me. The main focus is the baby on my grandmother's lap, a baby who, it turns out, is not a relative or anyone of great familial significance. My theory on how it endured is based on my own personal experience and practice of keeping photos where I look pretty and thin. And deleting all the rest.

Though I've never witnessed my mom do this, I have spent a lifetime watching her catch herself in the mirror and evaluate what she sees. On a recent visit, after not having seen me in a few months, she announced with shame, "You've probably noticed I've gained some weight."

I hadn't.

After my maternal grandma died, my mom sent me a photo album she'd curated from photos she'd found among Grandma's things. Most of the images consisted of my brother and me as children. But the last pages shifted into black-and-white: serious portraits of my grandma and grandpa as forty-somethings or younger. And then this one—an outlier.

My mother's beauty is the first thing I saw. Her hair is golden, stick straight and pulled into a tidy low ponytail. It might be the sepia quality, but she looks tan and unquestionably young. Until I sat down to write this, I'd barely noticed my grandma (arguably tied with the baby as the focus).

I hadn't really considered my mother's looks until I was about thirteen or fourteen and was snooping around some office drawers and came upon her wedding photos. (My parents had been divorced for so long that if these photos had ever been framed, I had no record of it.) I remember being shocked by the happiness behind her eyes, by her long dark-blond hair, which I assumed had always been short. I remember quite specifically thinking that she and my dad were a "glamorous couple."

CONTINUED

My mom and I have a difficult relationship. She's a doctor, a Republican, and a Christian in the WASP tradition—this means that she doesn't know how to hug with her whole body or sing hymns from the depth of her being. I'm a writer and a Democrat (if I must), and as far as religion goes, I recently read and loved a book titled *Making the Gods Work for You: The Astrological Language of the Psyche*. But this photo makes me feel something akin to empathy for my tight-jawed boomer mother.

It makes me think she must've come to realize at a young age that she was pretty and that her being pretty pleased people. When you're pretty, you often needn't say a thing to get a smile. Or a free drink. Or a second-round interview. I've heard this referred to as *pretty privilege*. And it *is*.

At the same time, it's what makes me feel for her, this woman no older than twenty, because I know that she's going to go on and on chasing this feeling that comes with quietly pleasing people, most of them men. She's going to spend a lot of time being good, or rather, making efforts to appear so. In the years and decades after her marriage fails, she will repeat to me the same sentence—"I thought I could make him happy"—in a tone that implies she still doesn't know why she couldn't.

I feel for this young woman because she's going to have a daughter who won't be won over by her thin frame and mascaraed lashes. She's going to have a daughter who will look at her like the mystery baby in the photo is: with scrutiny, warily.

Because she's going to have a daughter who is, I guess, not easy to please.

AMELIA MORRIS

C hristine *Platino*—wife to Rocco, mother of three grown girls—she isn't one for a fancy outing. Her nose wrinkles at the thought of getting zipped into an outfit, and she prefers stark-white sneakers and athletic ankle socks to any footwear in the world, especially a pair of pantyhose and a set of heels. Since I've known her, she's never swiped mascara on her eyelashes or blotted color on her lips or powdered her nose. I've never even seen a bottle of face moisturizer on her dresser. And her hair, untouched by dye or chemical treatment of any kind, has never been longer than my dad's.

And yet, on a late-summer evening in 1972, twenty-three-year-old Christine *Holm* wore a bold, orange, floor-length dress that cinched her waist and accentuated her dainty décolletage. Earlier that day she had her hair flipped at the salon and then carefully applied makeup to her sun-kissed face. The photograph was taken before she left for the date, and then, once developed, given to the young man who asked her to accompany him to his sister's wedding. That man was my dad, and the now-faded photo has sat in a frame on his armoire for more than forty years.

As a little girl, I didn't notice the picture more than any of the other ones scattered about our house, but as I got older and came to know my mother as the ultimate tomboy that she is, I would take it down and stare at it because I couldn't believe it was my mom! That pouf of amber hair! That shimmer around her eyes! That flirty smile! Who was that young lady? Certainly nobody I knew.

CONTINUED

It wasn't until I was nearly forty that I thought of that photograph again, when my eight-year-old daughter found a beat-up picture of me from my junior prom in a box of random keepsakes. She's used to my short hair, my big glasses, and my day-off uniform: sweat shirt, sweat pants tucked into my socks, and sneakers. The twisted updo, eyeliner instead of eyewear, sleeveless dress, and patent high heels must have bewildered her, for she stared at eighteen-year-old me with a punch-drunk smile for a long time. That night, I found the photo on her nightstand among her trinkets and knickknacks.

Since then, I've gathered more information about the night of the orange dress. I've learned that my mom went by herself to B. Forman's department store where she "for some reason fell in love with the tigerish pattern," that she had her shoes dyed to match, that her dad took the picture before dropping her off at the county club for the wedding reception date, and that she knew she would marry the man with whom she danced the night away.

Part of me wanted to keep asking questions and to know every detail of Christine's outing, but another part of me—maybe the part that holds tight to some of my own moments and memories like secret hints to a profound riddle—wanted to let her keep some wistful sentiments for herself.

LAURA SHIELDS

1972

1967

n this photo, my mother, Theodora Johnetta Lamond, is a senior in college. She has just been crowned homecoming queen and is riding on the float in the homecoming parade. She looks so regal and classy, which is what she was. Even as royal queen, she was approachable. That was her way: she had great wisdom and talent but was always humble. She made everyone feel like they mattered. After college she became an educator and used that same gift, connecting with people and mentoring so many.

I was my mom's caregiver for the last seven years of her life. After dialysis, she always wanted to go out to eat. She loved going to restaurants, especially on Sundays after church, and, in fact, those are my best memories of her: just talking and laughing over good food. She couldn't resist a prime rib. Now that she's gone, when I go to a nice restaurant with my husband, I think of her. I think, *Mom would have loved this place.*

NIKETA CALAME-HARRIS

My mother, Addie, was a photography major at a liberal arts college, and her love for standing behind the camera means she is rarely captured in front of it. Seeing photos of her from her youth is like finding an Easter egg, and her modesty means she's rarely the one to share pictures of herself with her three daughters, so much so that we've had to hunt them down from her close childhood friends. In this picture, my laid-back and soft mother is captured in the middle of her first New York City apartment; the fact that the kitchen supplies aren't stored in a drawer but instead are stacked on top of the fridge shows just how small and cramped the space was. I love her freckled and tan complexion, her eighties perm, and her even better eighties sweater. Today, she always knows the perfect time to laugh at a joke, although she is rarely the one cracking them. I imagine her here, caught like a deer in headlights, making everyone laugh. My mother may cringe whenever we look at this photo together, but she has nevertheless decided to keep it all these years. It must be a sweet memory for her to revisit.

GENNIE SIEGEL

1985

1965

This is my mother, Manibha, performing in the lead role of Rabindranath Tagore's dance-drama *Shyama*. It is 1965, and she is attending Calcutta Medical College. She is nineteen years old. In the play, Shyama is the most beautiful court dancer. When a visiting merchant that Shyama has fallen in love with is falsely accused of stealing a beautiful necklace and sentenced to death, Shyama asks another man who loves her to take the blame. When Shyama and the merchant run away together, he keeps asking her how she managed to free him from his predicament. When she finally admits the truth, he shuns her. My father, also a student at the medical college, was in the audience the night this photograph was taken. They had already begun seeing each other. She was breathtaking, he told me once.

Later, my mother worked as a pathologist at Wright-Patterson Air Force Base in Dayton, Ohio. She wore a light blue uniform shirt that showed her rank of lieutenant-colonel on her sleeve, and some weekends she would have to dress in combat fatigues and do military training exercises at various bases around the country. She would spend long workdays cutting through the fatty tissue of an amputated breast, or observing cells under a microscope, searching for malignancy, then be home in time to make dinner for my father, brother, and myself.

On weekends, from my time in elementary school until I graduated from high school, girls from the Bengali community would come over and she would choreograph dances from other Rabindranath Tagore plays for us to perform in rented high school auditoriums. She was so graceful, her hands able to twirl into the most delicate of shapes, but I couldn't see it then. I thought of her as provincial, limited, overly strict; nothing about her had the magic of creativity.

Now, as a forty-year-old woman—a mother myself—this photo takes my breath away. It's not just my mother's straight, slender arms, her thin waist, the sweep of her eyebrows and eye makeup, the smooth sheen of her skin, but the fact that she was a star, a consummate artist. That in this photograph, on that night, she transformed herself into the most beautiful woman at court, who could demand anything of anyone. How had I missed it all these years?

NEELANJANA BANERJEE

ven more than my mother's face, I love the whimsy in this photograph: the plastic flowers and knickknacks on her vanity, stripes of Philippine sunlight spilling through the blinds and echoing the curve of her body, how she holds the camera daintily above her head.

The stories I remember her telling me about her youth are stormier. How she hated her skin, darker than that of her eight siblings. How her legs were "ugly" and marked from so many mosquito bites. How, after graduating from nursing school, her father informed her that he was sending her to America to work and send money back. And how, when she decided to marry my father—a slobby med student with nice lips and a perpetually wrinkled lab coat—after just six months, jeopardizing her family's plans, my grandfather walked her down the aisle whispering, "This is nonsense."

Soon after she and my father arrived in America, she got pregnant and had a son. When it was time to return to the Philippines, she told my dad, who never wanted to emigrate in the first place, that she wasn't going back. She had another son and then, against her doctor's recommendations, a third child—me—because she always wanted a baby girl.

My mother and I are different people. I love my brown skin and my scars and am even less inclined toward filial piety. Our relationship has never been as easy as either of us would like. Right now she is deeply involved in the work of caring for my two young daughters, which means we are constantly fumbling our way through the intergenerational muck of family, obligations, femininity, presumptions. We misunderstand each other all the time. Recently, she asked me to lower my expectations of her.

In this photo I see the woman who willed me into being. I am here only because she insisted I be. The corner of my lip does the same upward curl. I'll never stop trying to connect, and I know I'll never be able to expect less. Look at her. How could I?

ANGELA GARBES

Early 1960s

Late 1940s

When I was six months old, my birth parents stole me back from the orphanage. My birth mother took me from New York to California because she wanted to find me a sunny home. She did.

I always knew I was adopted. My mom made me feel loved and special and safe. I've never known anyone as high-spirited and energetic. She was beautiful, tall, and thin, with bright blue eyes that had fire in them. This fire took her from Waterloo, Iowa, to singing in the USO, to marrying my father, to becoming a prominent citizen in Beverly Hills.

My mom was a passionate woman, a woman filled with aspirations. She was a perfectionist. She wanted everything perfect: her husband, her children, her home. She always dressed and put on her face, even if she was just staying home. She had her standards and expectations, and for that I'm glad. I learned to always try my best and not be ordinary. She hated ordinary. And so we all found our path out of ordinary.

CATHY WEISS

his photograph is of my grandmother Judith and my mother, Dalia. It was taken at my mother's Bat Mitzvah in 1963 in Jerusalem.

My mother's Bat Mitzvah was a huge event, which was unusual to do back then, for a girl. My mom thinks that maybe, because my grandparents never had a son (it was only her and her two sisters), they decided to make their first-born daughter's Bat Mitzvah a big deal. She told me it made her feel special. That, looking back, it felt like a feminist statement. In a way, it formed who she is today.

My mother remembers every detail: that my grandmother hired a famous tailor to come to the house and make a beautiful dress for my mother, and that she took her to the most famous hairdresser in Jerusalem back then, Max Ha Sapar.

Seeing this picture of my grandmother kissing my mother, on this most important occasion, touches me deeply. It's the love of a mother. The love my mother continues to pass on to me, now, long after her mother, my grandmother, has passed away. It's the strongest love of all, a mother's love.

When I tell my children how much I love them, my son tells me he loves me more. I always answer to him, "You can't love me more! There is nothing greater than a mother's love!" Then we argue.

But I do believe it.

I believe a mother's love is what makes this world bearable, possible. It's what we will not and cannot survive without. In a world of cruelty and pain, there is this one miracle: a mother's love.

Looking, almost going, back in time with this photograph, seeing my mother so young, a child to her own mother, I am filled with compassion and affection. There is something so vulnerable in both of them. We tend to forget the inner child that still exists in our parents, the child that, somewhere, they still are. I look at this picture and see my mother: innocent, longing for her mother's love, for approval and support on her big important day. A maternal sensation fills me . . . and as I feel for my children, I feel for her.

Now, when I see my mother, I also remember to see this girl in her, the girl from the photograph. She is still there, the same girl, my mother.

ELINOR CARUCCI

1963

Early 1990s

H ere are my mom and dad at their engagement party. They started dating when they were nineteen. My mom is from Queens and my dad is from Brooklyn, and they both ended up in Fort Lauderdale when they were teens. That's where they met—at a mall! In this photo, my mom is wearing her future mother-in-law's dress. My grandmother lent it to her for this special occasion.

ALYCIA ELIZABETH

love this picture of my mom and dad in the mid-1970s, taken in the garden of my dad's family home in Tehran. I love the way my mom is laughing here—how spontaneous it seems, how unselfconscious. And I love the tender way my dad is looking at her.

This picture was taken before my parents' lives were upended by the Iranian Revolution and the Iran-Iraq War. Before they had to immigrate to America with toddler me in tow and rebuild their entire lives from scratch. Here, my mother is still just a young law student, married to a newly minted architect, a bright future ahead of her. She doesn't know that she'll never get to be a lawyer. Or that she'll never again live in her own country, speaking her own language, surrounded by her family and friends.

My parents' lives in America have been defined by hard work and sacrifice. They raised two children, made mortgage payments, cared for and eventually buried their aging parents. My mom managed to work full-time, earn a master's degree, make homemade Persian food every night, and chauffeur my sister and me to myriad classes, activities, doctor's appointments, and friends' houses. It's no wonder that in many of my childhood memories, she's tired and worried.

CONTINUED

Mid-1970s

This picture represents another side of my mother. Her mischievous sense of humor, her kind heart, her zest for simple pleasures. Despite the fatigue and sometimes sadness I couldn't help but notice, she was a warm and playful parent, always making us laugh with funny voices, hand puppets, impersonations. Once every few months, she would let me play hooky from school and take me to the mall for Icees and Cinnabon rolls. She sang me to sleep every night with a song from my favorite movie, *Mary Poppins*. She did kind things for others: baking cakes for the neighbors, giving cash to homeless people, inviting in Jehovah's Witnesses for tea.

My parents now travel a lot, and my mom still makes friends everywhere: on airplanes, on trains, in Viennese cafés. She's good with babies and old people. She's great with puns, even though English is her second language. She loves finding little hole-in-the-wall restaurants and texting me pictures of what she ate. She regularly makes me laugh until I cry.

This side of my mom is what I love most about her and what I try most to emulate. If ever someone tells me that I'm warm or fun or funny, after I thank them, I always say that I get it from my mother.

PARIA KOOKLAN

t's hard to imagine my mother as a child. Even looking at this picture, in which she is a child, she does not seem a child. She seems herself: poised, even a bit regal, fully competent, graceful, loving, and grand. My mother, who couldn't have been older than eleven when this photo was taken, looks like my mother. The same full, gracious smile, the same beautiful skin, the same bearing. Her shoulder-length hair is pressed and braided into pigtails. She's wearing a bonnet: the photo must have been taken at Easter time. My mother stands close to her own mother, as she would continue to do for the rest of my grandmother's life. It wasn't until her mother had been dead more than a year that my mother finally did what she'd long wanted to do and started to wear her hair in a short-cropped Afro. The style sometimes brings her father into my mother's face.

I love how close she's standing to her mother in this photograph. She's actually set a little bit behind her family. Not like a shrinking violet. Instead, with confident security in her stance. I bet she'd already helped her mother accomplish some administrative task that morning—mimeographing church programs or folding bulletins—or maybe my mother helped get breakfast on the table, so her mother could type the last page of my grandfather's sermon. Even as a child, I think my mother must have been called upon to complete difficult tasks with a smile.

CONTINUED

Early 1950s

This photograph was taken in Lynchburg, Virginia, in the years right around 1952. My mother's family lived in a segregated neighborhood in a segregated town. There were white water fountains and colored water fountains. There were stores in which my mother and her family were not welcome to shop. The church my grandfather pastored was established 110 years before this photo was taken. Between 1879 and 1880, the building where he preached was built by the black laborers who worshiped there. By order of the deed for the building in which the city's public library was housed, my grandfather wasn't allowed to use those premises or its collection, so the members of Court Street Baptist Church started a library fund to help my black mother's black father buy the books he needed to preach the sermons his black parishioners needed to hear every Sunday in that deeply segregated, often hateful town.

I love this picture of my mother, with her people, on an Easter morning in the 1950s Jim Crow South, just miles up the road from Danville, Virginia, the last capital of the Confederacy. I can see in this photo the origins of my mother's deep pride and joy: her sense of connection with the people who love her and whom she loves. I know she's only a child in this photograph, but I recognize the love the girl in the photo radiates. It's the love I've always known, that I was born from and raised into. When she opens a door to me, she gives me that same smile. I don't know who held the camera that day, but her smile is for that person as well. Her smile has been the same for three quarters of a century. Look at the young girl's high, plump cheeks. She's still got those, too.

CAMILLE T. DUNGY

1983

've always adored this photo of my mother and father on their honeymoon. When they posed for the camera, they had no idea that they would create such a beautiful life for my sister and me. They recently celebrated their thirty-seventh anniversary, and I couldn't be happier to be a part of this family. My mother is a beautiful wife and an even more amazing mama bear. We would be lost without her. I hope one day I can be a fraction of the woman she is.

MEGAN JOY

Mid- to late-1970s

My mother, Sally, started her TV career as a five-year-old, climbing inside an old empty television and putting on shows to make her family laugh. She was whip-smart and thought she might become a physician like her father, until at the last minute she decided to go to theater school in Pasadena, California, leaving behind everything and everyone she knew in Portland, Oregon. She was a ringleader, a mischief-maker, and she loved to dance and sing. She told me she would scan the crowd at a party for the one person awkward and alone and try to make them feel special. She is the patron saint of castaways. I grew up in a house with seven bedrooms, which were always occupied with people who had nowhere else to go. Holidays were my mother's favorite. When I was five, she woke me in the middle of the night on Christmas Eve to see "Santa." She had hired a man to dress up, eat cookies, and deliver presents. Others were up on the roof stomping like reindeer. I peed my pants. When I was nine, my mom hosted a birthday party for herself and asked everyone to gift her with a drinking glass. A hundred people showed up, and our kitchen cupboard was forever filled with beautiful statement-piece water cups that LA's creative elite had scoured the city to find. In my twenties, my mom said to me, "I can't believe I gave birth to a hippie." I retorted, "I can't believe I came out of someone who likes air-conditioning and mayonnaise." I've never laughed harder with anyone than I have with my mother.

SAM RADER

W hen my mother first arrived in Washington, DC, she stepped out of Union Station, entranced by the cherry blossoms. Those pink-and-white flowers blooming from the trees must have looked like a technicolor Oz, far from the green moss and brown bayous of small-town Louisiana she'd just left behind. She was nineteen then and had never been farther than Texas; well-wishers advised her to not reveal that she was from out of town so she wouldn't get scammed. So she and her sister Liz jostled together in the back seat of a cab and acted unimpressed by all the sights—*Oh, just the White House? The Capitol? We've seen it all before.* But it must have been hardest for my mother to pretend to ignore the cherry blossoms. She told me this story once, years ago, and I like to think about my mother then, long before she was a mother, a woman I will never know. I like imagining her in the back seat of that cab, in awe of the world.

BRIT BENNETT

1970s

Here is my mom, at around twenty-one, studying opera in Italy. It's 1965 or '66. She's one of very few Japanese girls to have left her country and gone to Europe. See the confidence and style? She learned German, Italian, and French. She will forgo her career and turn her energy to me. She will teach me everything she can about her homeland, about beauty and art, and she will tell me every day, no matter how sick she becomes—and she becomes very sick—to never to give up.

MARIE MUTSUKI MOCKETT

1965 or 1966

1959

M y mother and I aren't crazy about this photo. It doesn't look like her, really—more like an idea of what a pretty girl *should* look like in the late 1950s. It's one of only two pictures she can find of herself (the other is even more artificial) before she gave birth to me at twenty-four, within a year of marrying a man she would divorce two years later. The photo was taken while she was on a picnic in Chicago with some fellow Marshall Field copywriters, the summer after she graduated from college. She was twenty-one. The photographer was a suitor whose ardor she did not reciprocate. Could those eyes be on the verge of rolling just a little? My mom is a beautiful woman, and in 1950s America, beauty like hers must have felt like destiny. I remember her telling me once that the purpose of her Vassar education was to make her a more "ornamental accessory" to whatever man she would marry.

I sometimes wonder what kind of life my mother would have had if she'd been born ten, or even five, years later. She would have pursued a career in theater casting, she says; she's been a theater nut all her life, and a devotee of culture and the arts. She is perhaps the only mother I've heard of who was actually *excited* to learn that her daughter wanted to become a fiction writer. Her own career didn't begin until the tail end of her second marriage, when she was in her early forties. She opened a modern art gallery in San Francisco and sold art for the next twenty-five years. She nurtured artists into vibrant careers and has nurtured mine from the start. Her life would surely have played out differently had she not been saddled with a two-year-old daughter when she exited that early marriage in 1965, at age twenty-six. But she has always made me feel that my arrival—and then my brother's—have been the great joys of her life.

JENNIFER EGAN

er parents called her Pennie, a name she hated because it made her feel worthless. Apart from that—and from her own telling—my mom's early childhood was happy. Her father was a newspaperman; her mother was beautiful. The house was filled with books, music, interesting people, and lots of alcohol. Then, in the same week that the atom bomb was dropped on Hiroshima, my grandfather walked out. My grandmother, who, even in the so-called happy days, had a mean streak, couldn't stop crying, blamed everyone—especially Pennie—for what had happened to her, and turned forever into an angry drunk and cruel woman. My mother was eleven, and she had nowhere to go, no way to escape. Oh, her father was *out there*. He had taken the books, music, and friends but not his daughter with him.

When my mother turned seventeen, Evil Grandma Kate, as we called her, married a man who was her equal: a mean drunk. He burned nearly every photograph of my mom and then kicked her out of the house. I always thought it was strange that my grandfather didn't take in his daughter, but he had bigger—or better—fish to fry. He'd become one of the earliest members of Alcoholics Anonymous and had married a woman so high up in AA that her story appears in the Big Book. No one had room for Pennie, and she went to live by herself in a furnished room. She relied on friends for food and companionship and to borrow sweaters, blouses, and skirts—perhaps even what she's wearing in this photo, one of a handful that exist before she married my father.

CONTINUED

Early 1950s

My mother put herself through school. She married when she was twenty, had me a year later, and got divorced two years after that. Sometimes we try to emulate our parents but fail miserably. Sometimes we try to escape them, and believe we have, only to find out we haven't. It comes down to that old question of nature versus nurture. I saw in my mother traces of Evil Grandma Kate, but my mom channeled her fury into her ambition and need for survival. It fueled her and kept her going when the world was saying she was worthless and unwanted.

From her dad, my mother embraced all that he'd taken with him back when she was eleven—books, music, and interesting friends. She wanted to be a writer like her father and in time would follow his advice to write a thousand words a day. (I'm now the third generation to do that.) By the time of her death nearly three years ago, my mother was no longer Pennie Laws. She was Carolyn See, the author of eleven books, a prominent critic, an esteemed writing professor, and considered by many to be the Grand Dame of Southern California Letters. A worthless penny had turned into someone admired and treasured.

LISA SEE

Growing up I used to wonder if I might be able to customize a time machine to carry me in time to my mother's arrival in Los Angeles, shuttling me back but also allowing me to up my age so I could be her "ace," the best friends we were meant to be.

Much of this wish was inspired by the stories she, an only child, would tell me about her years growing up in New Orleans. One that floats to the top is about her ritual of ferrying her toys onto her front steps. There, with a window dresser's care, she would arrange items—the paper dolls, the tiny tea sets, and whatnot—and wait as if onstage, hoping she might entice some passerby, some kindred spirit, with her carefully arranged bounty, her smile. I felt badly for my mother, and hence, the time machine, so that I could wander up those three steps and get lost in child's play. She never told this story to garner sympathy, and there is no photo to document it, but I think it was more of a measure—a check-in for herself about how far she'd come.

She captioned this photograph "Summer in Santa Monica" in white ink on black heavy scrapbook paper. In this image I see my mother's curiosity and enthusiasm. She's about eighteen here and has, it's very clear, fallen in love—with Los Angeles. My mother was far more extroverted than I tend to be. She sang, was a classically trained pianist,

CONTINUED

1950s

and studied drama. I see this in her eyes, too. An animation and intensity. As I examine her gaze, I wonder if she knows that this isn't just a summer detour. I wonder if she knows yet that once she graduates from college, she's not going back to New Orleans. That chapter is over, and somehow that little girl, who felt she had to coax company up three narrow steps to pass the time, had bloomed into something unforeseen. Did she know that she would find a vast and loyal cadre of friends—natives of this new place or transplants like herself? Did she know that she would coax her mother west, and her mother's mother? And she would try so very hard with her father, my grandfather, but he was as strong willed as he was wily. But that didn't mean that she would quit trying. I see this in her eyes, too.

I can't seem to square the lonely little girl on the porch with the young woman radiant in this photograph. What the "time-travel" of age tells me now is that she found not just a community but an essential part of herself here. Something that was activated. She loved Los Angeles—the hills, the ocean, the orange blossoms, the grand streets, its movie lore—but mostly it was the possibilities it offered. LA was a grand stage. She chose the mystery, not the familiar, a city that put everything on the future—as did she. That's in the smile.

LYNELL GEORGE

n this photo, my mother, Margaret, is seventeen, at Brighton Beach in Brooklyn, New York. This was when she worked for the bank president as his secretary. She told me he proposed to her—more than once. She always said no.

NANCY HIGH

1917

Everyone who knew my parents saw the easy romance they shared for forty-one years before my dad died of Lewy body dementia. My mom used to leave my dad notes and sign them with a doodle of a character she'd made up called Boog. In her wallet, she still carries a small card he made her that reads, "This card is good for an unlimited supply of 'I Love Yous.'" Walking behind them meant I'd probably have to see his hand over the back pocket of her jeans, so I often upped my pace. In most photographs from my childhood, their toothy smiles shine as they stand shoulder to shoulder behind me and my sister. In one of my favorites, they're slow dancing at a wedding: hands intertwined, eyes locked. In another, they're laughing as they hold up plastic cups of water to celebrate the end of a successful river-rafting trip.

In this picture, taken in 1966 while at San Diego State, my mom smiles at her college boyfriend. When I found the picture and asked about the guy in the white T-shirt, she said, "What's to say? We dated for a couple years. I was never in love with him." I'm fascinated by how this photo differs from so many taken of my parents. It's the overall dullness of her expression that I find most striking—her lukewarm smile and blank gaze, so unlike the enthusiastic and tender way she looked at my dad.

He's been gone seven years now. When my mom's friends encourage her to date, she says she had her love and it was true.

KRISTEN DANIELS

1966

1952

When this photo was taken, at a studio in Tucson, Arizona, my mother, Delia Villa Ferra, was just a sixteen-year-old high school student, working part time at a dry cleaner's to help support the family. She loved to dance and cook, and her favorite flowers were pink and red carnations. She was playful, mischievous, and very social. My aunt once said that walking down the street with her sister was like being in a parade: Delia waved to everyone.

She was also a loving, supportive, and fun mother. One afternoon when I was ten years old, she and I were sitting outside. My mom got the idea to smash grapes with our bare feet, just like they did to make wine in the old days. We were like that *I Love Lucy* episode come alive. We couldn't stop laughing.

BELINDA GABALDON

think my mother was in her late teens here, about ten years before she became a mother. Her siblings used to say, "Don't ask Sheila"; they knew that if they asked her opinion, she would tell them the truth without restrictions. She was scrupulously honest in her life and also in her behavior and judgments. Some of her opinions mortified my sister and me, but we knew, in the end, that she loved us.

ANN HOLLER

Late 1930s

1980s

My siblings and I never realized how much we all look like our mother, Denise, until we saw this picture of her: recently married and in her last year of college. We see ourselves in her eyes and mouth. We all carry a part of her, and in this photo, we see ourselves. But we also see her. She seems at once curious and shy, as if she couldn't wait for what life had in store but was also unsure of what lay ahead. It's like she hasn't figured out who she is yet. It's quite a contrast to who she is now: all confidence, sass, and joie de vivre. I want to go back in time to this moment and ask her what her dreams and aspirations were and what she wished she knew then. This is just a photo, but it's a reminder that no one is born a mother. We are all on a journey to learn and grow into ourselves over time. It is also a reminder that we don't have to have it all figured out by a certain age. And that the most important thing is to do everything with honesty, grace, and joy. This is who my mother was then (timidly so) and who she is now (loudly so): complex, a little haunting, and full of love and light.

NADIA AHIDJO-IYA

My mother, Angelica, is eighteen here—a college student in Manila who'd just switched her major from architecture to broadcast communications and started hanging out with an older cousin who taught at the university: an activist hippie, my mom says, who expanded her views on politics and art. (It's this cousin, named Bea, who took this photo and developed the film at home.) My mom and my dad had met in high school and were dating (very) long distance while he was in college in Toronto. They wrote letters to each other, which I remember finding in their closet when I was little. Back then I wasn't struck by how long my parents had known each other, or how no one ever knows anything about the future, or how easy it is to forget the possibilities that existed only in the past. I just remember thinking how beautiful both of their handwriting was: my dad's friendly and slanted, as neat as lettering in a graphic novel, and my mom's this near-abstract, spiky, rhythmic scrawl.

My mother is smart, musical, sentimental, curious, practical, tough, sensitive, concerned, solicitous, high-strung. In many ways the two of us move through the world very differently—what we have most in common may be the type of intimacy we establish with our best friends. But of course, so much of this difference is circumstantial. Sometimes I try to imagine my mom if she had been born the same year as me. Maybe she still would've gotten married in her mid-late twenties; almost certainly she wouldn't have quit her career to raise her two children, returning to work only after it was no longer the most important thing in her life.

In this photo, my mother is caught at a particular moment of collegiate possibility—she radiates the easy boldness of a young woman in an extended period of adventure, discovery, freedom. A decade later, she would effectively put those things in storage for me. I'm conscious of what might feel true for many children of post-1965 immigrants, for many daughters of this generation: it was my mother's willingness to place love over personal ambition that has made it possible for me to fear doing the reverse.

JIA TOLENTINO

1980

This is my beautiful grandmother Mercedes when she was dating, or just married to, my grandpa Al. When she was sixteen, she came from Puerto Rico to New York City with nothing and made a beautiful life for herself. She raised me, and she's one of the most selfless people I have ever known. I hope I become half the woman she is.

Unfortunately, she got dementia early on and is now in a nursing home. I show all the nurses this photo so they can see what a gorgeous woman she is.

NIKKI MERCEDES DIAZ

1963

I n this picture my mother is thirty years old. When she was ninety and a widow for the second time, this was the picture she dug out and put on the refrigerator of the house she was living in alone for the first time in her life. In the picture, she and her first husband, my father, have been married for eight years. Children of the Depression, they lived after their wedding with my father's family until they could pay cash for the house behind her, at 8020 North Poplar Drive in Milwaukee. My mother is working as a fashion illustrator for a large department store. She is converting to Catholicism with her best friend, Helen, who will be my godmother after my mother quits her job because she wants to have a baby. She and my father are still going to formal dances regularly with Helen and her doctor husband and their friends. The Depression is over, the war is over, everyone has a job, a partner, a home. My mother has a wardrobe of gorgeous formal dresses that I will assume all grown-ups have, when I am small and exploring her closet. In many, many ways this photograph captures a perfect moment in my mother's life.

The story she told about the picture was that sometime after it was taken, when she was off at work or maybe even after that, when she was pregnant with me, but certainly when she was not around, my father traded in this car, which she loved, for a stodgy Studebaker sedan. My mother would have made you laugh if she told you this story. (Even when she wasn't sure who I was anymore, she was so effortlessly witty she could make ER doctors certain she was completely cogent.) And this was the kind of story she liked to tell: wry, rueful, about how things go, especially where men are involved. I envied my mother's sense of humor, but there was almost always some bitterness in it. *You have to laugh,* she would have said. *What else can you do? You have to make the best of things.*

CONTINUED

1950

She was good, maybe even great, at making the best of things. She made sure to teach my sister and me to enjoy life's pleasures: hot coffee, good art, a well-made martini, conversation, and a story. She was charming. People thought she was better educated and better traveled than she was. She was fun to be with.

But she was also furious, the way so many women of her place and time were. It was a rage that was under the surface, that erupted when she was challenged or crossed. It was shocking, or at least it shocked me. She knew how to wound, and she never apologized. She didn't believe in it. It makes me sad to write this. She never got along with her mother, and she wanted us to be close, but that unnamed, unnamable anger was always in the way. I adored her, but in the same way she was always a little angry, I was always a little afraid.

I have another picture of her, at ninety-two or -three, looking at an enlargement of this picture and laughing. Her long white hair is braided, and she is still beautiful. Charming. Funny. Delightful. But never entirely knowable to the people—my stepfather, my sister, and I—who loved her. She was pleased that my husband had made this gift for her but not surprised. She knew her power.

In the black-and-white picture she is holding, the one she turned to, to be reminded of who she was, she is independent and sure of herself. In it, she looks back at the camera and my father boldly, a dark-eyed young woman who knows who she is and where she is. Who has her secrets and who will always believe it is better not to tell.

DARCY VEBBER

This photo was iconic in our family narrative. It's a still from a 1959 Hofstra College production of *A Streetcar Named Desire*. My mother playing Stella and my father Stanley. This is how they met. As a child, I was impressed by how glamourous, how larger than life they seemed, and it never struck me as odd that my parents were glimpsed in such an erotic embrace. I remember us watching the movie of *Streetcar* and teasing my dad until he bellowed "Stella!" just like Marlon Brando.

I also remember being proud of how lovely my mother was, as if that somehow reflected back on me. I thought of it when my daughter asked to keep a flattering photo of me at a similar age. I wonder if a girl can't see her own beauty until she discovers it in her young mother's face?

Now when I look at the photo, I am less interested in my mother's beauty and more interested in her expression. As Stella, she caresses Stanley, blissfully accepting his surrender. She is deep in her character, in her moment, in her acting. I know it was a great performance. She had big parts in all the plays she auditioned for. She won prizes; she was the "star" of the very impressive drama department (which, at the time, included fellow student Francis Coppola, who directed *Streetcar*). She had ambition to be a great actress and a movie star—she dyed her hair blond to look like Kim Novak. She studied at Stella Adler's studio in the city. I know how gifted she was, what potential she had.

CONTINUED

1959

My mother stopped acting after she got married. She had three kids instead. When you're in a family, from time to time it occurs to you that you never got around to asking your mom some big questions. Such as, why did you quit doing something you loved, something you were so good at? Finally, I did ask her, and she said she didn't hesitate at all. She was in love and wanted that middle-class life, wanted to be a homemaker. Okay, I said, but did you ever regret it? No, she insisted. We had so much fun in those early years with you kids. We were all so happy. But I wondered if this were true. Who could tell her children that she regretted having them?

As I age, I see these choices blur into themselves. Potential is hers to keep. Her acting, however not pursued, shaped her identity for the rest of her life. She is, to this day, a gently confident woman of deep empathy, curiosity, and intelligence. A beauty, too, with a disarming, unapologetic vanity. She has a star's electric presence. It is all still there, what acting gave her, and I begin to believe—to admire, really—the lack of regret.

DANA SPIOTTA

M y mother, Judith, at fifteen. A portrait of subtle clues—the contrasting aspects of her personality captured in a quiet, vulnerable way.

Her posture posed, neck swanlike but stiff. Her heart-shaped lips just barely offering a suggestion of a smile. Her warm eyes framed by the slightest eyebrow arch of challenge—only a glint—her self-possession distinct.

Cat-eye glasses and embellished daisy appliqué earrings. A soft scoop-neck sweater off the shoulder to feature her smooth skin and clavicle. Her hair short and efficient, confidence with a tight, curly bang.

She married her high-school sweetheart, my father, at nineteen. They alternated getting their graduate degrees while raising three children. A professional woman who worked eight-hour days, then came home each night to cook and clean and cuddle.

Ever insisting I "go dutch" on a date, my mother made sure to impart independence along with a daring urge. My first forays on stage were acting alongside her in community plays. She has been a fixture of fierce love in my life, most always soft, but sometimes hard—the balancing act of motherhood.

I have her same shape of clavicle; the same hazel hue of eye. The architecture of her bones I am proud to wear.

ANNABETH GISH

1956

1987

his is my mother, Laine, on her first day as program coordinator for the youth at the Haitian Catholic Center in Fort Lauderdale, Florida. I know she was smiling not because of her title but because she was able to make provisions for herself. As time grew, providing for one turned into providing for five. Thirty-two years later, she is now working in education and still finding ways to help the kids she engages with every day.

CASSANDRA TALABI

This is my mother, Robin, as she appeared around 1971. At the time, she ran a small natural-foods place called the Alfalfa Sprout on Long Island. The business didn't do very well. My mother has always been ahead of the times.

When I was little, I would stare at this photo, in awe of her beauty and lighthearted spirit. This photo was taken before her alcoholism, before her mental illness, and before being betrayed by two husbands. She looks so free.

ALLEGRA TAYLOR

Early 1970s

1970s

My mother, Moi Ling, was born in Malaysia in 1960, the second of eight children. When we're in Malaysia visiting her family, she reverts to her most instinctual self: talking loudly in Teochew, their dialect. There is no shortage of opinions, and they come at a deafening and relentless clip.

In America, where she and my father immigrated to with my younger brother and me when we were one and two, respectively, life was quieter and harder. While my father struggled to find a job, my mother took on odd hustles where she could: waitressing and sewing stuffed animals. She knew only the basics of sewing; she'd never waitressed before and didn't know the names of common cocktails because she didn't drink herself. She said yes to tasks she didn't fully understand and somehow managed to pull them off. I didn't know the name for it when I was younger, but now I realize what it was: *charm*. My mother was and is charming, and that charm, coupled with a determination bordering on stubbornness, went a long way.

Our younger selves couldn't have been more different. As a child, I must have puzzled her. I was an indoor kid who couldn't be pulled away from books. I dreaded running our weekly miles at school; even a lap was hard. My mother, though, excelled at all things athletic: She was a track-and-field star, especially good at the long jump. She was excellent at badminton. But the thing at which she was truly skilled was ping-pong. She had a mean smash. She was one of the two girls admitted to her math-and-science junior high; she was so good at ping-pong they wanted her on the school team. I love this photo of her, mid-smash, the rest of her life before her still. She'd approach it with this spirit intact.

RACHEL KHONG

took this self-portrait in 2010, three years before I became a mother, just a couple of months after my father died. I was feeling alone, and the most myself. I know this is not the assignment.

I recently asked my mother if I could use her photo for this project. She said no. I considered sharing one anyway, writing about her and her life. She might never speak to me again if I did— she isn't speaking to me as I write this. Still, I can't burn myself so brazenly. But I can write my own wishes. I can write fiction. I can pretend that my mother is a twin—the reason for my twin daughters—and that she first became a painter when looking at the sky over the Caspian, the air and water becoming one. She was one with it, too, and captured the feeling with paint on paper. I can pretend my mother was born with an extra toe—she calls it Baby and whispers to it when she's tired. My mother sings to me on my birthday.

Okay, here is one true thing: my mother has a laugh that is beautiful—loud, alive, and one that I still hear when I pull my bedsheets up to my ears, as if she were outside my childhood bedroom, in its now fossilized pink, entertaining her friends. Here is another: sometimes when I walk down the street at my most confident stride, I feel like she is inside me. For a split second, I am her. Maybe everyone feels these things. This also makes them easy to share. There is so much to tell that can't be.

One night recently, I thought, *What if I shared a photo of myself as a child?* If only the child me could talk to the child version of my mother, maybe we could understand each other. Maybe we could learn how to love each other. Now, we are rocks. Too hard, set, dry. But what if we were children again, softer? More like the water that flows out of the womb, out of the sky, new to the world, without history to mourn. Maybe in that state, we could even be friends. Of course, I know, even water has a past. Even rain came from the sea. But what if?

SANAM MAHLOUDJI

2010

1952

My mother-in-law, Alberta Marie Morris, was brought to California when she was three, after an odyssey that remains a family mystery. Her mother, Daisy Belle Morris, fled Mississippi as a teenager, after her own mother was killed. Daisy, whose radiant smile is replicated in Alberta's grin, had four daughters, anywhere from Arkansas to Oklahoma to Texas to New Mexico, until she finally arrived at her uncle's home in Calexico, California. Cousins remember that Alberta was already two or three then, but when she finally got a birth certificate, in her fifties, it read that she was born in the Golden State. Alberta and her three sisters were raised to work hard, laundering white shirts for businessmen and helping bake and deliver sweet potato pies famous in Riverside, California, all after school. The sisters were legendary for their beauty, and countless men tried to court them—but were held off by Daisy's own aunt, the fearsome Aint Dear, who timed their walks home from school, who asked sixteen-year-old suitors, "When you gonna cut some cake?" (The suitor who told me this was eighty by then and marveled that he had no idea why cake was involved.)

Those four girls had to be married young, for respectability and survival. Alberta fell in love, during her senior year of high school, with General Roscoe Conklin Sims Jr., a handsome Marine who danced with her at a party. In this snapshot, she is leaving for their wedding, standing in front of her mother Daisy's house, beside her fiancé's sister Loretta, who is only fifteen. Alberta is eighteen, ducking her head, perhaps laughing at something. She had graduated from high school two days earlier, in June 1952. Look at her shy smile, her regal bearing. She lived a few blocks from her mother's house, had her first child the following year, had seven children in total. My husband was her third son. Alberta taught me everything I know about being a mother—and a large print of this photo is in my living room. She lived a big life, all within three square miles, and yet there are hundreds of descendants from this woman, who, in this photograph, is so young, looking down at the slice of earth that is her mother's yard. She died too soon, at sixty-one, my husband having just whispered into her ear that I was pregnant with my third daughter, whose eyebrows and smile and dimple replicate Alberta's, so that she is here in the world now.

SUSAN STRAIGHT

My mother, Suzanne Sally Lingner, was an only child. Her mother was a cook for a wealthy family, and her father was a chauffeur for the same family. I remember a story she told me about her being home alone on Christmas while her parents worked. She also told me her father was an alcoholic. I think she had a lonely and sad childhood.

After she married my father, my mother became pregnant and lost the baby. She was unable to become pregnant again—and that was when they began the process to adopt my brother and, later, me.

As a mother, she was caring, soft-spoken, and very smart. She loved to read. She kept all kinds of articles and would store them in a special book. I will always remember her junk drawer in the coffee table in the living room, filled with papers of all kinds.

Here, in 1945, she has just graduated from the nursing program at Presbyterian Columbia Hospital. She is single. She will work as a nurse for only one year before giving it up to marry. I always wonder, if she liked being a nurse, why didn't she continue? I wish I knew what she liked best about her career. What was her favorite part?

CHRISTINE PLATINO

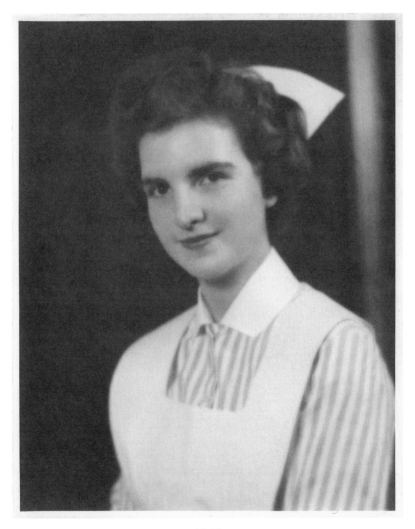

1945

2/12   FQ# @ 12 Hawthon Street. Aug. 1967.   Scott 3/97.

1967

The year is 1967. This is just before she met my father, before she had us three kids. It's a photo of before, but in truth it's also a photo of after. At twenty-seven, she is no ingenue, at the start of her journey. She looks already knowing, a little tarnished. She has already crammed in so much life. She has already made some major mistakes, with flair.

She has already gone west for college—and dropped out of college. She has already been married—and divorced. She has written and published two books of pulp fiction under a pseudonym—and has begun to write her first real literary novel. She has been voted Slum Goddess of the Lower East Side and dated pretty boy Eric Anderson, star of Andy Warhol's film *Safe*; she broke up with him after he slipped hallucinogens into her drink and sent her on a twenty-four-hour bad acid trip. She has already gone south in the summer of 1966 to report for CORE on civil rights violations.

CONTINUED

It takes work to find a patch of light outside my mother's shadow. Her stories, their myth-making quality, always leave me with this weary, jaded feeling, as if they happened to me. Women of her generation, I sometimes think, drank all the freedom juice, leaving none for their daughters. They lived so hard and so relentlessly that we, their children, have grown up skittish, cautious, demure, hemmed in.

At the park one day with my own kids, a mother friend tells me about a game called: What Would Your '70s Mother Do? It's an internet meme, a caution against helicopter parenting. It becomes a mantra between me and this friend after that. We say it over and over, laughing, trying to will ourselves to be as careless as our seventies mothers, so that we, too, will raise resilient, self-reliant children. We, too, want to chain-smoke and drag our children to protests and let them climb, unbelted, into the back space of the station wagon. We want our babies to suck on marbles and survive. We want to plow through lovers and multiple divorces. We want to care more for friendship than we do for romance. But we know even as we say it—*What Would Your '70s Mother Do?*—that it's too late for us; we know too much.

August 1967. Sometime after the bad drug trip, my mother left the Bowery. Moved back to her childhood home in Cambridge, along with the dog she called Woofer, a rescue from the Lower East Side SPCA. Her father was dead, and so was JFK. A friend, Laurence Scott, took this photograph. "This would have been before I met your father," she tells me of the photo. "The way I look in that photo is the way I felt," she says. "Lost." But what I like about the picture is that she doesn't look lost at all. She looks pissed off, a little louche, fired up and ready for more.

DANZY SENNA

V   ery early in life, I realized my mother was different
    from other mothers. She is a hurricane of emotions:
    when she's ecstatic, her laughter bellows, spilling
into the rest of the house. It's the same with her screams
when she's upset. My mother is complicated and misunder-
stood, whimsical and spirited. It simply depends on the day,
sometimes the hour. Throughout it all, fashion is her excuse
or her cure: a dangly earring, a gold bracelet, that perfect
scarf to tie an outfit together. A pair of elegant eyeglasses
gives her a reason to face the day.

Before I came along, the year was 1979, and my mother
had become a plus-size model for a spell. She was modeling
fur in a studio in San Francisco. Her perfect Afro frames her
face, her lips that memorable red I'd come to know throughout childhood. My mom was the only black woman I knew
who could rock this red—and she still wears it today. In
this photo she looks grand, special, and regal. A woman on
the go, to be seen, with places to be. Very married but still
available to dream.

I've seen this photo many times, but it's only now that
I realize how close my mother was to having a different destiny. Becoming a mother changed all that.

CONTINUED

I'm a new wife myself, and I recognize now how fast one's dreams can evaporate if you commit to motherhood above all else, even above your passions. That's what my mom did. It's why I'm struggling with the idea of parenthood for myself. I don't know how and when to suspend my ambition, and I'm not strong enough to think about it.

I've watched my mother's career dwindle with every decade. I always wondered if the struggle between us stems from hope lost. She decided to put her dreams to the side to have me, and then my sister. The ultimate sacrifice.

I've accepted my mother as human; she was whole, even before she gave birth to me. I've committed to absorbing her dreams and hopes. I've taken on the struggle for her, to create a reality that she never thought possible. I want to dock my mother's intensity at a safe port in a storm, in perfect weather. I want her to walk in fashion, in vogue, confidently, captivating the world with her grace, magnetism, and heart.

It took me thirty-nine years to realize she's the love of my life and the one I have always been looking for. She built the ship that I sail.

WYNTER MITCHELL-ROHRBAUGH

1979

1969

My mother grew up in poverty in the Vietnamese countryside after all the men in her family were killed by the Viet Minh. Forced into an arranged marriage to an abusive man, she gave birth to a son when she was only fourteen. This picture is from after that. There are no pictures from before she was a mother.

She ran away to Saigon with her first child. When he became ill and she couldn't find work, she returned to her village and left him with her mother. Her ex-husband soon came and took the child away. My mother searched but was unable to find him. She began to build a life for herself in Saigon, supporting herself as a maid and teaching herself English.

Eventually she met my father, an American Navy officer. They married and had six kids, of which I am the youngest. When I was three years old my father tracked down my brother in a Cambodian refugee camp and brought him to live with us in Rhode Island. We didn't know he was our brother; we thought he was just a Vietnamese refugee. It wasn't until I was fifteen that I learned the truth.

I remember how scared she looked when she told me. She was so afraid that I would judge her for abandoning her child, that I would think she was a bad mom. As if that thought was even possible. As if I had not spent my whole life watching her do whatever it took to protect and nurture our family.

When I was in junior high, she went back to school and earned her GED, then her associate's degree, then her bachelor's. She started telling people her story, and after twenty years of working on it she recently published a memoir of her life in Vietnam, *Crossing the Bamboo Bridge: Memoirs of a Bad Luck Girl.*

I thought I knew how amazing she was, but I had no idea. Reading her story, I finally understood the depth of her pain and the magnitude of her strength. No one should ever have to go through what she went through. She survived a war and somehow found peace. She has always been and will always be my greatest inspiration. A little woman with a big heart. Before. Now. Forever.

EIRENE DONOHUE

This was taken when my mother, Lalita, was nineteen or twenty, in India. She would eventually move to the United States, where she attended graduate school for immunology, met my father, had two children, and made scientific discoveries the girl in this photo probably did not think possible. I love this picture because before anyone had any idea what she would accomplish, she already looked so fearless and full of life, traits that middle age and motherhood have not changed.

MAYA RAMAKRISHNAN

Late 1970s

My mom moved to San Francisco in the 1960s and lived there most of her life.

She loved to throw parties: parties that got her and her roommates evicted when she was in her twenties, parties with the Winterland roadies, parties with themes like Come as You Aren't and Spam. She taught me how to throw parties, too, and every year we hosted a Christmas craft class at our apartment.

She had all sorts of jobs, from secret ice-cream taster at Baskin-Robbins to secretary at *California Farmer* magazine. She was proud to be the fastest typist in the typing pool at Southern Pacific Railroad. She owned her own store called To Be Continued on Sacramento Street in Laurel Heights, demonstrated cooking in woks for Taylor & Ng, and had her own edible bread sculptures business. She sold collaged rocks and jewelry she made from typewriter keys at local craft fairs, and for forty years she was the personal assistant to prominent psychiatrist Jack Dusay, MD. Half Chinese and half German, my mother proclaimed herself Lady Nona Wong Kline, CAP (Chinese American Princess), and had business cards printed to prove it.

There was no one else like her. I always admired the way she didn't care what people thought of her and how she made people laugh. She had style. She sacrificed a lot to raise me by herself, and I will always be grateful that she raised me in The City.

NYSA WONG KLINE

1966

1968

Here is my mom, Leslie, in 1968 when she was twenty-six years old and living with my dad in Chicago. He was getting his PhD in physics, and she was finishing up her last year as a third-grade teacher before getting pregnant with my older brother. She would take time off to stay home with him. (I came three years later, after they'd moved to Colorado.)

Mom is a driven, ambitious, and deeply responsible person, but she also has a carefree side that comes through in this photo. Here you see her whimsy, her artistic spirit, her charm. Her smile is beautiful. The wind is in the waves and in her hair. Here is a young woman in the Windy City about to get rocked by the biggest decision of her life: the decision to become a mother. She could not have foreseen the discipline, dedication, and exhaustion that accompanies new motherhood. Who can? Still, she assumed the role like a natural. She took us around the world, showed us how to express ourselves artistically from a young age, instilled in us her deepest values of respect for others and for nature, and cooked us three balanced meals, day after day, year after year. She continued all this caretaking even after she went back to teaching when I was a first grader. Did she feel it was a grind? If so, she didn't show it. Is she a saint? Of course not.

Looking at this photo, I want her to know that she's right to be hopeful; that although her life will be filled with challenges, she'll meet them with a fortitude I'm not sure she knows dwells within her.

LAURA VEIRS

Until two years ago, I had never seen pictures of my mom before she lived in the United States. When I finally saw this photograph, I was astounded. This is Minh, in Vietnam, as a teenager. The year is 1970. In a country ravaged by war and under strict Communist rule, here is my mom rocking it in a minidress. I love this picture because I can finally put a face to the girl in all the stories she told about her childhood. This is the girl who got into fights with boys, started her own business, and won awards for her storytelling. She became pregnant with my oldest brother around this time, and despite all the hardships that were to come, this bright, vibrant, loving girl has never left.

TIFFANY NGUYEN

1970

Alberto

1988

This is my mom, Elisha, at her junior prom back in 1988. She was seventeen. One of the biggest songs that year was "My Prerogative" by Bobby Brown, and I can only imagine her feeling the beat by swaying her hips and snapping her fingers. I like to think she and her date, Johnny, cut it up on the dance floor.

I'm mesmerized by her electric smile in this picture. Her dimples are so pretty. She looks so innocent. But I know this seemingly carefree teenager had already seen so much darkness and known far too much pain. She would have already experienced sexual abuse numerous times and had been the victim of an abduction. It sounds like too much to comprehend, let alone to live out. Her life in those first seventeen years was much more complicated than it should have been.

But then again, that electric smile sums up exactly who my mother is: a superwoman with unparalleled courage and strength. That, despite the horrific experiences behind her and the fear of the unknown in front of her, she was determined to change the narrative of her story. She's still smiling today, and wider than ever, because she did manage to change that story. I couldn't be any prouder of her for it.

JASMIN PETTAWAY-SOLANO

My mother is an artist, and I love this picture of her: lost in creating something, nestled comfortably with her tools, focused on her project. I love how bold she was to take colored markers or pens or pencils into her bed with white sheets, wearing a white outfit.

When I saw this photograph for the first time, I had a moment of supernatural discomfort, because in it, she looks so much like me. That was the structure of my thought, not "I look so much like her" but "*she* is *me*," which I think (hope!) was not a narcissistic slip but instead me opening up my life and inviting my mother to inhabit it with me.

The picture reminds me of a story my maternal grandfather, now passed, told me about my mother. It wasn't a story about a specific moment in her life but an explanation of her character. When my mother was a teenager they would get into epic fights, screaming battles. My grandfather would send her to her room, but she would continue to argue the whole way up the staircase and shout at him from the top of the stairs.

When Grandpa told me this, a vivid memory came back to me like a shock: standing on the staircase in my childhood home and screaming at my mother. I felt time and space fold, until there was no difference between my mother as a teenager and myself at the same age. My mother and I are very different people, so I love every moment that I feel similar to her. I treasure most deeply the times when I've felt that we were not different in any way, at all.

CATIE DISABATO

1984

Here is Julia at seventeen, being photo-graphed by her dad in their front yard in Flint, Michigan, only hours after her graduation.

She's smiling. How promising the future looks! With high school over, finally, *finally,* she's standing on the brink of her dream to become a singer—a great singer.

On this bright day in 1927, years of piano lessons, singing lessons, and countless hours of rehearsal on the upright piano in the parlor are behind her, along with performances around Flint, which have garnered local admiration. (She can hit an E above high C, and her rich, contralto voice has been compared to Marian Anderson's.) Behind her as well is that scary but triumphant vocal audi-tion for the Westminster Choir College in Dayton, Ohio, where soon she will begin her professional training. Everything is in place. She's on her way!

As the camera makes this happy moment indelible, Julia can't foresee that within months of arriving at school, and while still a teenager, she will meet Ray, a handsome young salesman for National Cash Register. Though conflicted, she will marry him, give birth to my sister, and then her dream of becoming a singing star will sink forever into the black hole of domesticity.

CONTINUED

1927

Her husband's life will become her life, isolated from the musical community she cherishes; her singing aspirations will be narrowed to church choirs, and she won't have a piano to play for the next eleven years.

Ray will become successful and provide her with material comforts, which she will enjoy; she'll love gardening and bridge club; she'll be a good mom to my sister and me. But these activities will never compensate for the loss of her chance to become a singer.

Since she'll be without encouragement or even musical colleagues, over time Julia's skills will atrophy from lack of use.

Her regret will remain intact.

Later, when I attain a degree of television celebrity, she'll be pleased with my success, but it will be only secondhand pleasure. She had yearned for something more, a success of her own. Toward the end of her life she'll say to me, "Oh, Barb, how I wish I'd had the opportunities you've had."

I wish she'd had them, too. Who knows what mark she might have made? What remains is this photo, a bittersweet record of that shining moment when Julia's dream was still alive.

BARBARA FELDON

W ithin a week of arriving in Europe with the Christus Rex church choir from the University of North Dakota, the group unexpectedly disbanded. The priest chaperone drank steadily, the doctor chaperone disappeared behind the Iron Curtain, and the pastor told the students to just meet up again in Brussels in six weeks. My mother, Jill, and her best friend, Jodie—nineteen, from a tiny town in the northwest corner of Minnesota, and flat broke— picked up their bags and started hitchhiking. The first man to pull over drove them to Frankfurt and kindly gave them a room, but in the middle of the night came the inevitable knock on the door and "Fraulein, fraulein, let me in." When my mother barricaded the door with furniture, he gave up. The next day he took them to Amsterdam and pointedly dropped them off in the red-light district. They found a woman who rented out rooms and had a son in a rock and roll band; they hung out with the band for a while, "a crazy trip."

This was 1972. My mom and Jodie were living on five dollars a day. They would lurk around restaurants, waiting until people left their tables, and then they'd grab the rolls and run. At a French monastery where you had to pay to shower, they scaled a wall and climbed in for free. In Geneva they hopped a train and sneaked into a first-class private compartment with red velvet seats; along the ride, a

CONTINUED

1972

distinguished gentleman joined them without saying a word. When the porter came and asked for their tickets, they knew they were about to get kicked off—until the man spoke to the porter in perfect French and he let them be. The man turned out to be the Turkish ambassador to the United Nations.

As far as her parents knew, and still know, she was touring with the choir the entire time. "Things were looser then," she says. At nineteen they were expected to be able to navigate the world on their own and figure things out, and they did.

Two years later, my mother married—one of the last people in her class to wed, at the seasoned age of twenty-one—and the year after that, she had me. But that singular adventure stayed with her. "You know, somewhere in your heart aren't you always nineteen? Where you have that completely fearless approach to life and everything is a possibility? Always, even at age sixty-six, there's still that part of me. Sometimes you forget about it, but it's always present. You always miss that a little bit. Maturity is one of the most disappointing things in life."

CHELSEY JOHNSON

never knew my mother, Tawny Ochs-Choi, to stand this
way: so tall, radiant, embodied, quietly powerful. I remember what it felt like to wrap my arms around her legs. I
remember my mother, my shelter, bending over my young
self, then, a few years later, over my sister. She's retained
the shape of her shelter, subtly, the sometimes-tired curve
of her spine, a marker of her motherhood, a bulwark against
unpredictability, things out-of-control, her body a capsule
for her mother's death and my father's rage, holding on to
survive, holding on for love, holding on as habit.

Here she is, in 1983, four years before she became my
mother. My father's shadowed face peeks out from behind
her. This was when she believed she mattered, before she
began giving everyone else the benefit of the doubt and
before she began shrinking herself to make room for others.

This was—and is—my mom, my pride. She is as brave
and worthy as ever.

ASH CHOI

1983

1977

My mother the summer before she begins her senior year of high school: this girl is sitting for her graduation photos, just having removed the cap and gown—not the real ones yet, just the prop ones the studio owns. The photographer has asked her to slip her bra straps off her shoulders and wrap this fuzzy faux-fur thing around herself. Velcro keeps it closed. He promises her it won't look as cheesy in the finished photos as it does in real life.

She'd plucked her eyebrows clean away so as to be able to draw them in as she pleased. She says it was the style then, in the late 1970s. Less the style, more just her: she'd cut her hair this short for the first time the week before the scheduled photo shoot, an act of rebellion and the only one afforded her, as she'd yet to leave her home on a date without a chaperone despite being, in this photo, less than a year away from not just graduation but also her wedding. On the day of this photo, she'd already been engaged for two years.

Her mother wanted to kill her for cutting her hair so short right before school pictures.

But this girl would go on to do the exact same thing the week before her wedding day. *That* cut—even shorter—was an attempt to dodge the antiquated skullcap her mother had picked out to hold her veil. This girl wanted a crown of flowers instead, but her mother had said no. With days to go, she cut her hair so short that she was sure pinning in the skullcap would prove impossible.

She was wrong, though. They found a way to secure it. So it's only in this picture, this graduation one, that she exudes pure triumph. I always thought of it as her movie star picture; as a little girl, I'd look at it and pretend she'd been on her way to becoming someone famous—because this was also her mother's story; Abuela had been a singer in Cuba before the Revolution. This framed eight-by-ten hung in my abuela's house until, my abuela gone and the house sold, I took it down to hang it in mine.

JENNINE CAPÓ CRUCET

J ust weeks before my mom, Agnes, was to serve as the muse for the social club Lucena Varsitarians' annual ball, her father passed away. He had been suffering from coronary thrombosis, which affects blood flow to the heart, and was kept in an oxygen tent at the hospital. My mom was at his bedside when he died. Despite her grief, she had no choice but to attend the ball as planned, having her hair and makeup done and donning the gown made especially for her. She had been selected to be the muse the year prior, and it was considered a great honor in her town.

My mom has always had to balance social obligations with her family's needs. This juggling act started with being born into a Filipino family with eight other kids. It continued through her teenage years and later, when she mothered three daughters in the States, and persists even today, now that she's in her seventies. My sisters and I call her out on this all the time. Maybe we're just being selfish—but shouldn't family come first? I've come to realize, though, that she has the capacity to give so much to so many. What may seem to be a struggle from my point of view is not from hers. She believes she can do it all: be the dedicated daughter, the amazing sister, the supportive wife, the caring mom, the doting *lola* (grandmother), the social butterfly, and even the town muse. And she'll move worlds, cross continents, and drive on multiple freeways all night long to be there, for everyone.

Our family recently returned from a weeklong medical mission to her home island of Marinduque, which my mom organized with her large network of friends, Filipinos and Filipino Americans alike. We brought free medical care to six towns, from complimentary dentistry to cataract surgeries, serving thousands of residents. And there was my mom, each day, at the center of the action. On this trip, I was truly able to embrace that, for Agnes, being a mother isn't her end-all. Perhaps back in 1963, the social club saw that this seventeen-year-old would become someone others would aspire to be and be inspired by. The perfect muse.

TEENA APELES

1963

1940s

My mom grew up in a rural and very remote area of northeastern Washington, and she was a country girl through and through. As a little girl, she would fish from the nearby creek to help put food on the table. She also knew how to hunt from a young age. Though the game she hunted was always small (squirrels and grouse, mostly), she was an impressive shot. She's a woman with grit but also so much gentleness, which I think this photo shows perfectly. Even in her work clothes, she's still absolutely stunning. I also love seeing her long black hair up in braids. After she had children, she always kept it short. She became a mother of seven children and is now a grandma to thirty-seven grandchildren and sixty-five great-grandchildren!

HEATHER EKINS

My mom, Holly, has been a flight attendant at Delta Airlines for more than forty years and still works for them. She's waited on passengers who smoked cigars, or who spit out tobacco in plastic cups that she had to clean up, or who hit on her after one too many Jack and Cokes. In the early days, she got weight-checked and had to wear degrading uniforms, including high heels for ten hours straight—in the air. In an ingenious move, she bought ugly teeth at a joke shop and, to avoid harassment, she wore them when the male passengers would get too wasted.

I have never met anyone who has taken so much pride in their job. She has such camaraderie with her friends she flies with. They fly to Thailand and, on their layovers, take cooking lessons. They travel through sacred temples in Japan, and tour monuments in Manila, and drive through the countryside in Ireland. They never stop learning.

I'll never forget a day in kindergarten. It was Bring-Your-Parent-to-School Day, and it was designed to introduce different careers to the class. When I came in from recess my mom and her best friend, Mary Jane, greeted my entire class at the door. They handed us fake tickets and welcomed us aboard. They had rearranged the classroom to look like an airplane and carefully helped us to our seats and took our coats. Once we were seated, they served us red or white (grape juice) and handed us peanuts and playing cards and then gave us the instructional routine. Our six-year-old minds were blown. I know that every kid went home that night, proudly wearing their plastic gold-painted wings, and told their parents they wanted to work for Delta when they grew up.

MOLLY SCHIOT

1971

1958

A fter my father and his first wife divorced, my mother helped my father take care of his children when he was working, becoming a mother figure to them. I guess one thing led to another, because before long they were pregnant with me! The story of our family is special to all of us: it's as if we chose each other, siblings and stepsiblings alike.

Aside from staying home with us, my mother helped my father with his business. For additional income she also did sewing jobs—upholstery, curtains, and clothing. She loved it, and even through our childhoods she nurtured her own aspirations. Every month or so, we would drive to her best friend Elaine's apartment in Philadelphia (we lived in New Jersey at the time) to spend the weekend. They would talk and smoke cigarettes and design clothing and sew, and we would occupy ourselves: play, color, watch TV, and draw. I see now that that was a nice break for her and Elaine, who was a single mom of two teenagers.

My mother recently celebrated her seventy-ninth birthday. She loves to laugh, loves to disparage most political leaders, and she doesn't miss a thing. She has strong intuition. She is appreciative of manners, cordiality, and kindness. She loves flowers, art, fine music, good TV, good food, sewing, crafting, creative projects, and good company, and she abhors rudeness and racism. Although my mother is very "light skinned," with light green eyes and blondish (now white and blond) hair, she is very much a black woman and proud of it! She has the ability to be old-fashioned and completely modern and up-to-date at the same time. She keeps up with her ten grandchildren and six great-grandchildren through social media, text messages, and phone calls. She prays for us all the time, and her prayers go straight to God. I know it!

KIMBERLY DURDIN

G rowing up, whenever my mom saw I was upset that something wasn't going my way, or whenever I complained about some rule she made me follow, or something she didn't let me do, she'd say, "When I was fourteen, my friend Sue invited me to a Beatles concert in New York, but my parents wouldn't let me go." My mother often told me this tale throughout my childhood. It was a rebuttal when I complained about her and my dad's parenting choices, or when I was dealing with a frustration of the teenage variety: not being allowed to stay out past 11 P.M., a strict ban on co-ed sleepovers, no tongue piercings until I was eighteen. Other times she talked about it wistfully—what could have been. She, a shy, quiet teen from a small town in New Hampshire, had been invited by a friend's family to fly on a commercial plane to New York City and see John, Paul, George, Ringo, and their soft mops of hair—*in person*. But her parents, adhering to the strict New England WASP code of conduct to never impose on other people even when invited to do so, refused to let her go. Even decades later, the injustice of it all was always implied, her disappointment palpable.

When I started seeing Phish shows as a teenager, my mom—the kind of protective parent who cautioned against driving on "wet leaves" because they were as dangerous as black ice—let me head off down the highway in a friend's dad's station wagon, chasing my musical idols for days at a time all over the East Coast. It didn't dawn on me until much later that maybe her memory of being refused her teen self's greatest dream influenced her parenting in ways I never realized or appreciated.

Recently I found her old high school yearbooks. Inside were gushing messages from her friends all about the Beatles, complete with mentions of that concert in New York, verified in faded blue ink that still seemed to pulse with promise and excitement.

I don't know where this photo of her falls on the timeline of things. Was it taken when she thought she was going to experience the big city and the Fab Four, or was it snapped later, when the sour taste of parental letdown and unrealized hopes had set in? Either way, I love her in it; her face has that perfect teenage mix of skepticism and hope, brimming with disappointment but also the possibility that something amazing might just happen to her at any second.

KATE SPENCER

1960s

Early 1940s

My mother had a traumatic childhood, and it left her wise and melancholic. Born premature, she wasn't held by her parents for weeks because the doctors were scared that, like her twin brother, she wouldn't make it. For the rest of her life, she'd wonder: If she'd been held in those first few weeks, would she still feel as though something was missing?

When my mother was nine years old, her own sweet mother died of a heart attack. After that, she and her older brother were separated and sent to different cities around the Deep South to live with relatives, because it just wasn't right to leave two children with a widower, not in the late forties. Then her father remarried and she lived with him again, but in a tumultuous household marked by her stepmother's verbal abuse. My mother was unflaggingly gentle, sometimes to the point of disappearing. I once caught her hanging up the phone with a sheepish look, and when I asked her what she was doing, she admitted she was sending flowers to her stepmother for her birthday, a woman so excised from our lives I'd never met her. At the time, I told her she shouldn't send the flowers, but now I see the generosity and the way it probably helped my mother slip out of the noose of resentment.

CONTINUED

Sometimes I wanted my mother to fight back, to let fire rage through her, but anger was not her motivator or even, really, in her emotional lexicon. Instead, she was eternally tired. In some ways, I became her spirited defender, if only in my mind. If someone wronged her, I held the rage for my mother until the fire burned my hands. It also meant that during the years I was angry at her, I breathed in nothing but smoke and ash. How could I defend my mother against myself? The position I was trying to play, that of loyal protector, wasn't mine to carry out.

When she died, I went searching for this picture, a rare happy moment from her childhood. She's two and a half here, hanging on to her grandparents' old dog, looking off in the distance, already knowing. I like to think that in that moment, crouched close to her grizzled mutt, she felt safe and protected from anything that would come her way.

MARGARET WAPPLER

W / hen I was in my teens, strangers always remarked that I looked "especially mature" for my age. This explains how I was able to pop nonchalantly into our corner liquor store next to the Alpha Beta grocery to stock up on wine coolers for our high school theater cast parties when I was only fifteen.

People used to say the same thing about my mother, Elizabeth "Maria" Katindig, a jazz singer born to a *bourgeois-bohème* family of musicians who is credited with innovating Latin jazz in the Philippines. When I look back at pictures like this, I know what those folks meant, because my mom must've only been around seventeen or eighteen when someone snapped this picture of her and Eartha Kitt after she and her band opened for the legendary singer at a swanky supper club in Manila in the early 1970s.

My mom was only eighteen when she had me in 1973, so I, like all the other onlookers in my early childhood who marveled at her preternatural poise, had no idea what an actual *baby* she was. Indeed, "Baby," was how I heard people refer to her the most when I was first sentient enough to notice my mother had a nickname.

Whatever tension and closeness we have now stems largely I think from this series of semantic misunderstandings swirling around and between us—between "Ayen" (my infantile

CONTINUED

Early 1970s

pronunciation of my own name) and "Baby," between me and her—from the moment I was born to this good Catholic girl who got married just seven months prior. She was a baby who herself had a baby. I find it almost poetic that she's pictured here, in her full youthful glory, with Eartha Kitt, a woman who owes at least some of her iconicity to a swinging Christmas song with "baby" in the title.

To top it all off, my mom's nickname "Baby" was spoken as a kind of honorific to most eldest daughters in Manila, thus infantilizing her (and all others who carry that nickname), while also saddling these women with a compulsory sense of family leadership and responsibility. It is that tremendous burden, that responsibility to the entire clan, that my mom still carries with her now, decades after she mothballed those gowns and eventually began trotting around in matching REI fleece with my dad instead, all the while pursuing a second—nay, *third or fourth* career—selling real estate in the Inland Empire of Southern California. She gave up the glitz, the glamour, the literal rubbing-of-elbows with powerful women like Eartha Kitt to take care of me. To take care of all of us.

KAREN TONGSON

M y mom knows how to bodysurf, whistle, catch a pop fly in baseball, ride a unicycle, water-ski, roller skate, and play the accordion. She's my first phone call regardless of whether I've had a great day or a terrible one. This is her at twenty-six years old, at a baby shower thrown by her friends, looking forward to the next adventure (which just so happened to be me). It's how I always imagine her: happy, armed with great hair and relentless optimism. She is forever looking forward, excited to see what's going to happen next. I've had many wonderful successes in life, but my greatest stroke of luck was getting her for a mom. She's my best friend, but I'll never be as cool as her.

ROBIN BENWAY

1977

My mom was twenty-four and in nursing school in Louvain, Belgium, when she traveled to Italy with her roommate, Gaby. I imagine their guttural French like static against the lilt of Italian, their bright faces turned toward the coastal light.

Not long after, Gaby convinced my mother to go to a New Year's Eve party specifically because there would be a pack of raucous Americans there. At midnight, my mother sat on the lap of one and they kissed. Three years later, she dared herself to get a job as a nurse in New York and tracked him down. That was my father. They've now been married fifty-six years.

Gaby also immigrated to America decades ago with her then-husband. She and my mom have always kept in touch, but this past year she has flown across the country several times to reminisce. When they talk, the girls they were spring back up, still meeting, after fifty years. They lapse into the argot of their life as nurses, splice English and French into a polyglot franglais only they seem to understand.

I think of the years in between, of suburban housewifery in Miami, where my mom was the center sun in our lives, the chief enabler of my dad's medical career, and the long chain of hours between school drop-off and pickup that she alone filled.

I think, too, of her upbringing, how she was born in Rwanda to Belgian parents. How she moved back to Brussels before eventually emigrating alone to risk love in the *sauvage* US, barely speaking English. There is an outsiderness that my mother has experienced all her life, part of it an embrace, part of it a shield.

People have always asked my mom where she's from, her accent like a coat she can never take off. Though so many years ago, this trip represents something about her that is invisible, but essential, to her identity and my perception of her. It's a self who is daring and adventurous, ecstatic to experience the zest of first adult freedom, who felt that anything she wanted would be possible.

ELLINE LIPKIN

1960

1960

She said she didn't like being famous. Born mixed-race in a country long associated with the persecution of its "minorities," she'd submitted to the world of Burma's beauty pageants and celebrity as a service to her disadvantaged family. What was harder than the tabloids' slander, she said, was the loss of unself-consciousness: before she'd been well-known, she could fall asleep on a public bus without being photographed, eat noodles on the side of the road without strangers saying she would gain weight. But she was a rebel and, young as she was, found a way not to forfeit artlessness alongside anonymity. You see her smile here, its unabashed openness, even as fans trail her? That was the smile—more than a decade later in America—in which I first gleaned what acceptance and honesty, strength and vulnerability, might look like. That was the smile—as I grew into the awkward self-consciousness of childhood, when people assumed she was my nanny—which could make me want to rush to her defense. From others, I learned the games of shame and self-hiding: diets and sarcasm and reserve. But she happily put on pounds and remained herself. Movie star, minority, refugee, foreigner, warrior—she played her roles lightly, as if to say: "What does any of it matter, when, together, we remain?"

CHARMAINE CRAIG

his is my mother, before she was a mother, when she was just Leslie. It's one of the few pictures I have of her pre-me, as in, an actual photo that I have somehow managed not to lose in the seventeen or so times I've moved since I left home. She's standing in front of the Golden Gate Bridge on a trip to San Francisco she took with my dad before they were married. I like to look at it and imagine us meeting not as mother and daughter but as two white wine-, turquoise-loving people in the Bay Area. I wonder if we'd become friends.

Growing up, we didn't have what I'd call an easy time getting along. Most close to us said it was because we were so similar—just about the worst thing you can say to a sixteen-year-old who constantly vows to never be like her mother. Now that I'm older, I can say with certainty—and humility—that both my best and worst traits are her carbon copy, which in retrospect might have made for too much of a good thing (or just too much of . . . something). Now, I'm grateful for our similarities. It took a long time (and a lot of therapy!), but we have finally found each other's rhythm, both of us much softer and more patient with each other. What helped was trying to remember that before she had me, she was just a person in the world, doing the best she could, like we all are, like I am now.

ALISON ROMAN

1984

T his is the only photograph my mothers could find of themselves together prior to having children. And that fact in and of itself speaks to their story perfectly. My mothers, Robin and Russo, met in 1979, fell in love instantly, and three months later were trying to have babies. Using a known donor who was a gay man, Russo inseminated herself using a glass syringe with no needle. My older sister, Cade, was born in 1980, and as my mothers describe it, "She was so perfect we wanted to do it again right away." So they went about finding another gay man who was willing to donate his sperm and contribute to the making of a lesbian family during a time when such a thing barely existed. They wanted to use gay men as donors because they suspected other gay people would understand their family better. Robin inseminated herself with the sperm of a different gay man and gave birth in 1981 to me, Ry Russo-Young. They hyphenated our names to reflect both of their identities and the equality of their union. My mothers weren't artists, but I like to say that their greatest creation was their family.

RY RUSSO-YOUNG

1979

ere is my mother, Helen Chung-Hung Hsiang (1937–2014), along with two of her classmates at what was then called Mount Mercy College in Cedar Rapids, Iowa. My mother is on the right. It is 1956, and she is nineteen years old.

She was born in Shanghai only weeks before the Japanese invaded the city. After moving twenty-six times during the Sino-Japanese War, her family left China for Macau and then Taipei. Studious and shy, she was profoundly changed by the loss of her father when she was seventeen. Because her own mother did not attend even primary school, my mother had to navigate the world without the advice or support of a worldly parent. She was admitted to Wellesley but did not have the money to attend, and came to Mount Mercy College as one of several Chinese scholarship students. There, guided by the Sisters of Mercy, she majored in English literature and psychology. On weekends, the international students were introduced to nearby Iowa City and to the Amana Colonies, where they ate creamed corn and mashed potatoes. On weekday evenings, my mother took long walks through the residential neighborhoods of Cedar Rapids, gazing into the picture windows, longing for a home.

I'm pierced by my mother's innocence and by her beautiful smile. She did not believe that she was beautiful. She grew up in a culture where beauty was measured by paleness, daintiness, and shoe size; by these standards, she was too tall, and her size-seven-and-a-half feet so large that her shoes had to be special-ordered. She lacked confidence in her looks, but in this photograph, she is dazzling.

LAN SAMANTHA CHANG

1956

About the Contributors

NADIA AHIDJO-IYA is an African feminist and mother of two living in Senegal.

TEENA APELES is an LA-based writer and editor who founded the publishing collective Narrated Objects. She is also the mother of a prolific storyteller.

NEELANJANA BANERJEE is the managing editor of Kaya Press and teaches writing at UCLA and Writing Workshops Los Angeles.

BRIT BENNETT is the author of *The Mothers*.

ROBIN BENWAY is a National Book Award–winning author of six novels. She lives in Los Angeles.

NIKETA CALAME-HARRIS is the voice of Young Nala in *The Lion King* (1994).

ELINOR CARUCCI was born in Israel and now lives in New York. She is an award-winning fine art photographer whose work has been exhibited worldwide.

JADE CHANG is the author of *The Wangs vs. the World*.

LAN SAMANTHA CHANG is a novelist in Iowa City, Iowa.

ASH CHOI is a psychotherapist and consultant in Seattle, Washington.

CHARMAINE CRAIG is the author of the novels *The Good Men* and *Miss Burma*.

JENNINE CAPÓ CRUCET is the author of the novel *Make Your Home Among Strangers*, the story collection *How to Leave Hialeah*, and the essay collection *My Time Among the Whites*.

KATE CRUM is a broadcast engineer in Bloomington, Indiana.

KRISTEN DANIELS is a writer living in California with her husband and two daughters.

NIKKI MERCEDES DIAZ lives in New York City, works in tech, and loves dogs.

CATIE DISABATO is the author of the novel *The Ghost Network*.

EIRENE DONOHUE is a screenwriter and mother originally from Rhode Island and currently living in Los Angeles.

CAMILLE T. DUNGY is an editor and author. She has published eight books, most recently *Guidebook to Relative Strangers*.

KIMBERLY DURDIN is a midwife, lactation consultant, and co-owner of KindredSpaceLA, a birth, lactation, and education center in Los Angeles. She is the mother of six children and a grandmother of three.

JENNIFER EGAN's most recent novel is *Manhattan Beach*.

HEATHER EKINS lives in Colville, Washington, next door to her mom. She is a mother of four herself.

ALYCIA ELIZABETH is a college student living in South Carolina.

BARBARA FELDON wrote *Living Alone and Loving It!* and played Agent 99 in the TV series *Get Smart* (1965).

BELINDA GABALDON has two kids: a stepson who's almost twenty and a son who's eight. She lives in Los Angeles.

ANGELA GARBES is the author of *Like a Mother: A Feminist Journey through the Science and Culture of Pregnancy*. She lives in Seattle.

LYNELL GEORGE is a journalist and essayist based in Los Angeles. She is the author of two books, *No Crystal Stair: African Americans in the City of Angels* and *After/Image: Los Angeles Outside the Frame*.

ANNABETH GISH is working hard to juggle the roles of mother/actress/writer/director.

MARGARET GUZIK is a mother of five and grandmother of seven. She was born and raised in New Jersey and enjoys traveling the world.

NANCY HIGH is a retired nurse, first responder, mountain rescue person, a mother of six, grandmother of fifteen, and great-grandmother of twelve.

ANN HOLLER is a writer and former editor and researcher who lives in Los Angeles.

CHELSEY JOHNSON is the author of the novel *Stray City* and lives in Flagstaff, Arizona.

MEGAN JOY is a spa director in the Baltimore, Maryland, area.

RACHEL KHONG is a novelist living in San Francisco.

NYSA WONG KLINE is a daughter, wife, mother, only child, native San Franciscan, amateur fine bookbinder, compulsive photographer, aspiring artist, private pilot, Francophile, and cat person who has worked in the international wine industry for twenty years.

PARIA KOOKLAN is a nonprofit fundraiser living in Southern California with her husband. She talks to her mom at least once a day.

ELLINE LIPKIN is the author of a book of poems, *The Errant Thread*, and a nonfiction book, *Girls' Studies*.

LAURA LIPPMAN is the author of more than twenty crime novels.

SANAM MAHLOUDJI's fiction appears in *Timothy McSweeney's Quarterly Concern* and the *Kenyon Review*. She's at work on a novel.

FRAN MELMED is pretty sure her daughters haven't yet considered her life as a Mother Before. She celebrates her mom and all girls with grit as the founder of JMB Award.

WYNTER MITCHELL-ROHRBAUGH is a displaced San Franciscan, digital strategist, podcaster, writer, daughter, sister, and stepmom living in Los Angeles with her loving and patient husband, Allan. Tweet her at @wyntermitchell.

MARIE MUTSUKI MOCKETT is a writer living in San Francisco. Her most recent book is *American Harvest: God, Country, and Farming in the Heartland*.

AMELIA MORRIS is the author of the memoir *Bon Appétempt* and the cohost of the podcast *Mom Rage*.

VALLERIE MWAZO is currently pursuing a master's degree in Chinese medicine. In her spare time, she enjoys traveling and movement therapy.

TIFFANY NGUYEN is a nonprofit professional living in Omaha, Nebraska.

KIKI PETROSINO is the author of three books of poetry, most recently *Witch Wife* (Sarabande, 2017).

JASMIN PETTAWAY-SOLANO is an Emmy Award–winning TV producer from Cleveland, Ohio.

CHRISTINE PLATINO and her husband have taken up traveling as their retirement hobby and always send postcards to their grown children and grandchildren.

SAM RADER is a psychologist and perfumer in northeast Los Angeles.

MAYA RAMAKRISHNAN is a law student at the University of Washington.

ALISON ROMAN is the author of the cookbooks *Dining In* and *Nothing Fancy.*

RY RUSSO-YOUNG is a writer/director and lives in Los Angeles with her family.

MOLLY SCHIOT is a director living in Los Angeles.

LISA SEE is the author of numerous international bestselling novels, including, most recently, *The Island of Sea Women.*

DANZY SENNA is the author of five books, including the novels *Caucasia* and *New People.*

LAURA SHIELDS is a screenwriter moonlighting as the GM of a popular restaurant in Los Angeles.

GENNIE SIEGEL lives in Brooklyn, New York, and is currently campaigning to become the favorite daughter. Results still pending.

SHARON SMITH is a retired neuropsychologist who has lived with her husband in Maine for nearly fifty years. She enjoys gardening and both reading and writing mystery novels.

KATE SPENCER is the author of the memoir *The Dead Moms Club* and cohost of the *Forever35* podcast.

DANA SPIOTTA is the author of four novels: *Innocents and Others*, *Stone Arabia*, *Eat the Document*, and *Lightning Field*. She is the daughter of Emy Frasca and the mother of Agnes Coleman.

SUSAN STRAIGHT's new memoir, *In the Country of Women*, was published in 2019 by Catapult. Her novels include *Highwire Moon*, *A Million Nightingales*, and *Between Heaven and Here*, all featuring mothers and daughters.

CASSANDRA TALABI lives in Southern California and teaches kindergarten.

ALLEGRA TAYLOR is an early childhood consultant in Cambridge, Massachusetts.

JIA TOLENTINO is a staff writer at the *New Yorker* and the author of the essay collection *Trick Mirror*.

KAREN TONGSON is the author of *Why Karen Carpenter Matters* (2019) and *Relocations: Queer Suburban Imaginaries* (2011). She is a professor at USC and coeditor of the award-winning book series Postmillennial Pop (with Henry Jenkins) at NYU Press.

DARCY VEBBER lives and writes about marriage, family, ritual, and Judaism, in Hollywood, California.

LAURA VEIRS is a singer-songwriter. She lives in Portland, Oregon, with her husband and two sons.

MARGARET WAPPLER is the author of the novel *Neon Green*.

CATHY WEISS is an artist, educator, and mother living in Laurel Canyon, Los Angeles, with her husband and two dogs.

MOLLY WIZENBERG is the author of *A Homemade Life*, *Delancey*, and *The Fixed Stars*.

Acknowledgments

The wonderful people at Abrams get all the credit for making this book so beautiful. Thank you to Liam Flanagan, Annalea Manalili, and Deb Wood; of course, extra special thanks go to my editor, Rebecca Kaplan.

Thank you to my agent, Erin Hosier, for all her enthusiasm and hard work, and for her many, many good ideas regarding this book. Thank you as well to Chris Gelles for lending his talents early on when this idea only existed online and in my head.

This book would not exist were it not for the Instagram that started it all—and the Instagram would not exist were it not for its contributors. Thank you to everyone who has shared their mothers' stories and photos with me and the world. You brighten my inbox and my day.

I am so grateful to the contributors to this book. Your talent and vulnerability and humor amaze me! You're amazing! Thank you for making this book so meaningful. It's *all* you.

Last, I'd like to thank my family, especially my mother, Margaret Guzik, and the three terrific human beings who made *me* a mother: Dixon Bean Brown, Ginger Dean Brown, and Mickey Ocean Brown.

Editor: Rebecca Kaplan
Designer: Deb Wood
Production Manager: Rebecca Westall

Library of Congress Control Number: 2019939746

ISBN: 978-1-4197-4294-1
eISBN: 978-1-68335-887-9